40
days in

MARK

Titles in 40 Days Series

40 Days in 1 Samuel
40 Days in Mark
40 Days in Psalms (release March 2021)
40 Days in 1 Corinthians (release March 2021)

40 days in

MARK

WILLIAM F. COOK III

PUBLISHING
NASHVILLE, TENNESSEE

Published by B&H Publishing Group
Nashville, Tennessee

Dewey Decimal Classification: 242.5
Subject Heading: DEVOTIONAL LITERATURE / BIBLE. N.T.
MARK—STUDY AND TEACHING / CHRISTIAN LIFE

Cover illustration by bweetRenie/shutterstock

1 2 3 4 5 6 • 23 22 21 20

Contents

Preface vii

Day One: Jesus Christ, the Son of God 1

Day Two: The Kingdom Inaugurated 7

Day Three: Blasphemy and Bad Company 11

Day Four: Controversies Continue 15

Day Five: An Expanding Ministry 19

Day Six: Family, Accusations, and Followers 23

Day Seven: Kingdom Parables 27

Day Eight: More Kingdom Parables 31

Day Nine: Kingdom Authority over Nature and Demons 35

Day Ten: Desperation and Faith 39

Day Eleven: Penetrating the Darkness 43

Day Twelve: God of the Impossible 47

Day Thirteen: Graceless Religion 53

Day Fourteen: Jesus Does All Things Well! 57

Day Fifteen: Overcoming Spiritual Blindness 61

Day Sixteen: Life's Most Important Question 65

Day Seventeen: Mountaintop Glory and Real-World Ministry 69

Day Eighteen: Service, not Self-Seeking 73

Day Nineteen: Marriage, Children, and Possessions 77

Day Twenty: A Peculiar Kind of Greatness 81

Day Twenty-One: The Triumphal Entry 85

Day Twenty-Two: When Jesus Gets Mad 89

Day Twenty-Three: The Patience and Judgment of God 93

Day Twenty-Four: Jesus on Government and Marriage 97

Day Twenty-Five: Loving God and Neighbor 101

Day Twenty-Six: A Study in Contrasts 105

Day Twenty-Seven: Jesus Predicts the Destruction
of the Temple 109

Day Twenty-Eight: The Destruction of Jerusalem
and the Return of Christ 113

Day Twenty-Nine: Be Ready! 117

Day Thirty: Devotion and Treachery 121

Day Thirty-One: Preparations for Passover 125

Day Thirty-Two: Jesus' Body and Blood 129

Day Thirty-Three: The Darkest Night of All 133

Day Thirty-Four: Jesus' Betrayal and Arrest 137

Day Thirty-Five: Jesus before the Sanhedrin 141

Day Thirty-Six: Peter's Denials 145

Day Thirty-Seven: "Suffered under Pontius Pilate" 149

Day Thirty-Eight: The Crucifixion of the Son of God 153

Day Thirty-Nine: At the Cross 157

Day Forty: The Resurrection of Jesus Christ 161

Notes 165

Preface

Forty is an important number in the Bible. Moses was on Mount Sinai with the Lord God for forty days (Exod. 34:28), Elijah traveled for forty days before arriving at Mount Horeb (1 Kings 19:3–8), and Jesus was tempted in the wilderness for forty days (Mark 1:13). Some self-help experts believe it takes forty days to develop a habit. Whether they're right or wrong, there is no habit more important for a Christian to develop than a consistent devotional life.

In *40 Days in the Word*, readers will discover a humble attempt to assist believers longing for a fresh moving of God's Spirit in their life. This series intends to enable believers to read though books of the Bible in their devotional time discovering God's truth within its biblical context. The Spirit of God uses the Word of God to mature believers in their faith and increase their passion and zeal for Jesus Christ.

Many Christians find it difficult to sustain momentum in their devotional life. They desire to read the Bible consistently but lack encouragement, guidance, and direction. Commentaries are often too technical, and devotionals may fail to challenge them to dig deeply into God's Word. The *40 Days* series offers both a deeper discussion of a biblical passage and at the same time encourages the reader to make personal application based upon what the text *actually* says.

We live in a day where casual Christianity (which is not biblical Christianity at all!) has infected the church in the West. People are clamoring for shorter sermons that are more focused on felt-needs rather than on the Bible, and many in the pulpits are obliging. Furthermore, the songs that are often sung fail to extol the greatness of God, but instead make people feel better about themselves and their comfortable lifestyles.

If the church in the West is to recapture the passion of the early church, God's people must spend time on their knees with their Bibles open allowing God's Spirit to convict them of their sin, build them up in their faith, and empower them to take the gospel across the street and around the world. The hope of the authors of this series is that God's Spirit will use these volumes to help God's people develop an ever-increasing love for their Savior, Jesus Christ.

In addition to helping individual believers, the series holds out hope for small groups desiring to focus their meetings on the study of the Bible. A group would spend approximately two months (five days of readings per week) reading through a book of the Bible along with the *40 Days* volume, and then base their discipleship time encouraging each other with what they discovered during the previous week.

The Spirit of God and the Word of God work together to strengthen God's church. The apostle Paul put it this way: "Let the word of Christ dwell richly among you, in all wisdom teaching and admonishing one another through psalms, hymns, and spiritual songs, singing to God with gratitude in your hearts" (Col. 3:16). Paul's hope is my prayer for you as you journey through these next forty days.

Bill Cook
Holy Week, 2020

Jesus Christ,
the Son of God

Mark 1:1–20

The Big Picture

Mark begins his gospel at "break-neck" speed. In the first thirteen verses, he introduces the main character (Jesus Christ, the Son of God), describes John the Baptist's ministry as the fulfillment of ancient prophecy, and depicts Jesus' baptism in the Jordan River and temptation in the Judean wilderness (Mark 1:1–13). He then moves from a summary of Jesus' message ("the kingdom of God") (1:14–15) to a description of the call of his first four disciples (1:16–20).

Digging In

The opening verse serves as both an introduction to the book and a Christological confession (1:1). Mark starts at "the beginning." For Mark, the beginning of the gospel about Jesus is the ministry of John the Baptist. The word *gospel* means "good news." The good news is about Jesus Christ and the salvation he secures.

1

The main character in Mark's gospel is Jesus Christ. The name *Jesus* is the Greek equivalent of the Hebrew *Joshua*, which means "Yahweh saves." The Greek term "Christ" is the equivalent of the Hebrew "Messiah." Both words mean "anointed one."[1] "Son of God" is an important Christological title for Jesus as well. The title is used about Jesus by demons (3:11; 5:7); by God at Jesus' baptism (1:11) and transfiguration (9:7); and by a Roman centurion at the climactic moment when Jesus dies (15:39). Another reference to Jesus' Sonship is in the high priest's question: "Are you the Son of the Blessed One?" (14:61). Strangely enough, the title "Son of God" is never used by the disciples in this gospel.

John the Baptist's ministry was foretold in the Old Testament (1:2–3). The phrase "as it is written" is a standard expression indicating the authoritative nature of the Old Testament. The reference to Isaiah refers specifically to the second part of the quotation in verse 3; while verse 2 is a reference to Malachi 3:1. Mark refers only to Isaiah because he was the more prominent of the two prophets. John did not appear "out of the blue," but he was clearly a part of God's redemptive plan.

Mark applies Malachi 3:1 and Isaiah 40:3 to both John the Baptist and Jesus. The Baptist is both "my messenger" and "a voice." The phrase "prepare your way" in verse 2 is paralleled by "prepare the way" in verse 3. John prepared the way for the coming Messiah by his preaching. The imagery in Isaiah is the return of God's people from exile. Mark takes a passage in Isaiah that refers to the coming of Israel's God and applies it to Jesus.

John's ministry took place in the Judean wilderness. People flocked to him in this barren wasteland (1:4–8). John's baptism was the most characteristic aspect of his ministry. His baptism symbolized repentance from sin. Repentance refers to a change in one's thinking that results in a change of lifestyle. John's preaching created quite a stir as people journeyed to the wilderness to hear him and be baptized by him. His appearance and lifestyle were reminiscent of Elijah (2 Kings 1:8; Mal. 4:5–6). John's clothing was common to nomadic desert dwellers. His food ("locusts and wild honey") was not unusual for people living in the desert. The locust was akin to a large grasshopper.

At the heart of his message was a person, the coming Messiah. John recognized his inferior role to the coming one. He acknowledged that the Messiah was mightier than he and that he was "not worthy to stoop down and untie the strap of his sandals." Untying someone's sandals was the task of a common slave. John's baptism was with water, but the coming one would baptize "with the Holy Spirit."[2]

Jesus' baptism marks the inauguration of his messianic ministry (1:9–11). God's voice at his baptism confirms Mark's earlier statement about Jesus being the Son of God. Jesus came to the Judean wilderness from Nazareth, which was a small town in Galilee located about half-way between the Sea of Galilee and the Mediterranean Sea. As Jesus came up out of the water, "he saw the heavens being torn open and the Spirit descending on him like a dove." Mark emphasizes the immediacy of the events. This is the first of Mark's forty-one uses of "as soon as." The term heightens dramatic tension and movement in the narrative.

As Jesus came up out of the water, "he saw the heavens being torn open." The imagery is of God in heaven tearing open the sky below as he prepares to act. The same word is used at Jesus' crucifixion in reference to the temple veil being torn (15:38). At the beginning of the gospel, at Jesus' baptism, God tears the heavens open, and at the end of the gospel, when Jesus dies, God tears the temple veil from top to bottom. Jesus' messianic ministry begins and ends with these heavenly acts. At his baptism, he identifies with sinners, and at the cross, he dies for them.

Jesus saw the Spirit descending upon him. The probable background is God's work at creation. Genesis 1:2 says: "And the Spirit of God was hovering over the surface of the waters." If this imagery is correct, then the thought is that Jesus' ministry is the beginning of a "new creation." Furthermore, his ministry will be empowered by the Holy Spirit.

Jesus alone appears to hear God's voice. The first part of the pronouncement reflects Psalm 2:7, which is a coronation psalm used at the installation of Israel's kings. Therefore, Jesus is identified as God's Son and Israel's true king. The second part of the quotation is a reference to Isaiah 42:1, which is a part of the first of Isaiah's Servant Songs, identifying Jesus as the true Servant of the Lord. At the inception of

Jesus' messianic ministry, God declares him to be his beloved Son and Israel's Servant-King.

One should not miss the Trinitarian nature of Jesus' baptism. God the Father speaks words of affirmation and love; the Holy Spirit descends on Jesus to empower his messianic ministry; and Jesus, the divine Son, is baptized in the Jordan. Jesus' baptism at the beginning of his public ministry points toward its culmination in his death, burial, and resurrection.

Jesus goes directly from his baptism into conflict with Satan (1:12–13). Mark's description of Jesus' temptation is extremely brief when compared to Matthew 4:1–11 and Luke 4:1–13. The brevity of the description makes it more striking. Unlike Matthew and Luke, Mark does not describe any of Jesus' temptations. Mark describes the Spirit driving Jesus into the wilderness. The point is that Jesus was not caught off guard by the encounter, but it was a part of God's plan for him.

The "forty days" are reminiscent of the forty years Israel wandered in the wilderness (Num. 14:34). Mark highlights the fact that where Israel failed as God's son, Jesus was obedient and victorious. Mark alone makes reference to the "wild animals." The thought adds a greater sense of danger to the scene.

Jesus' ministry begins officially after John the Baptist's imprisonment (1:14–15). Mark's comment, "the time is fulfilled," is reminiscent of Paul's statement in Galatians 4:4: "When the time came to completion, God sent his Son, born of a woman, born under the law." Jesus proclaimed "the gospel of God;" that is the good news from God and about God. At the heart of Jesus' gospel preaching is "the kingdom of God."[3] The kingdom of God refers to God's rule or reign rather than to a geographical realm, more a power than a location. The kingdom was inaugurated with the coming of Jesus and will be fully manifested and consummated at his return. The requirements for entrance into the kingdom are repentance from sin and faith in the gospel.

Jesus' method of kingdom expansion is discipleship. The setting of verses 16–18 is the Sea of Galilee, a body of water that is approximately 8 miles wide and 13 miles long at the farthest points. Jesus approaches four fishermen, calls them to follow him, and says he will make them "fish for men." They immediately leave their profession to follow Jesus.

Living It Out

As significant as John the Baptist is, this passage is about Jesus Christ. Mark's understanding of Jesus' identity is stunning: Jesus is the long-awaited Messiah, God's Son. His forerunner was prophesied in Israel's sacred scriptures. He identified himself with those he came to save at his baptism and was pronounced by a voice from heaven to be God's beloved Son. His ministry would be empowered by the Spirit, yet the rending of the heavens at the beginning of his ministry and the tearing of the temple veil at the end is often overlooked. These two events bracket Mark's gospel. At the beginning, God acknowledges Jesus as his Son, the very one who will cry from the cross, "My God, my God, why have you abandoned me" (15:34). Truly, this Jesus is to be loved, worshiped, and followed.

The Kingdom Inaugurated

Mark 1:21–45

The Big Picture

Today's reading details the beginning of what is known as Jesus' early Galilean ministry. Capernaum, situated on the northwest shore of the Sea of Galilee, is both the launching point and the base of operation for Jesus' Galilean ministry (Matt. 4:13). In just a few brief paragraphs, Mark describes Jesus' ministry moving from obscurity to tremendous popularity. The section is punctuated by references to the growing crowds (Mark 1:28, 33, 37, 45). By the end of the chapter Jesus has to spend time in unpopulated areas due to the size of the crowds. Furthermore, the passage demonstrates how Jesus will advance the kingdom through preaching, healings, and exorcisms.

Digging In

After calling the four fishermen to be his disciples, Mark describes Jesus teaching in the Capernaum synagogue (1:21–28). Those in attendance are stunned at the authoritative nature of his teaching compared to the teaching of the scribes. Unexpectedly, an unclean spirit (demon) in a man recognizes Jesus as "the Holy One of God." While the disciples and crowd do not know Jesus' true identity, the unclean spirit certainly does.

The demon fears that Jesus has come to destroy them. This is the first of four major exorcism stories in this gospel (5:1–20; 7:24–30; 9:14–29). Jesus silences the demon and commands that it come out of the man. The exorcism was somewhat violent as the demon causes the man to go into a convulsion, and it screams as it comes out of him. The crowd is amazed at both Jesus' authoritative teaching as well as his authority over the demon. The news about Jesus begins to spread widely throughout Galilee (1:28). Jesus' presence is an assault against Satan's dominion. As the kingdom of God advances, the prince of this world will fight back but the outcome is already a settled issue.

Jesus departs the synagogue and goes to the home of Simon and Andrew accompanied also by James and John (1:29–31). Jesus heals Simon Peter's mother-in-law of a fever. She immediately gets up and begins to serve them. After the sun sets and the Sabbath regulations concerning work end, the entire town gathers at the door. He heals many who are sick and casts out many demons (1:32–34). Jesus would not allow the demons to speak because they knew his true identity. Jesus silenced the demons so they would not identify him publicly and thereby keep messianic speculation as muted as possible. Many Jewish people looked for a militaristic messiah who would throw off the yoke of Roman domination.

The next morning, Jesus rose very early and went to an isolated place to pray (1:35). Mark does not describe Jesus praying often in his gospel, but when he does, it is at crucial moments (6:46; 14:32–39). Mark clearly indicates that prayer was an important part of Jesus' life. Each reference comes at a time when Jesus made important decisions about his ministry. Here he must decide if he will remain in Capernaum and let the crowds come to him or if he will take the gospel outside Capernaum. The point is that crucial decisions in life should be saturated in prayer. When Simon does finally find him, he exclaims,

"Everyone's looking for you!" Jesus' agenda, however, will not be determined by the disciples, or the crowds, but by the Father.

Jesus and his four disciples leave Capernaum and make a tour throughout Galilee preaching and "driving out demons." The only event that Mark describes during this initial tour of Galilee is the healing of a man with a serious skin disease (1:40–45). In Mark's mind, this event must have been very important, since it is the only one he records out of all the sermons Jesus preached, the people he healed, and the demons he cast out on this tour of Galilee.

The man had a serious skin disease called leprosy. The Old Testament gave specific instructions in Leviticus 13 and 14 on how those with leprosy were to be treated. The man believed Jesus was capable of healing him, but he was uncertain if Jesus was willing. Jesus was "moved with compassion" and reached and touched the man and healed him. Interestingly enough, Jesus did not have to touch the man to heal him, but his touch demonstrated his compassion toward him. The man had probably not felt a human touch in a long time.

Several things may be in play here. First, it was believed that only God could heal leprosy and, that is exactly what Jesus does. Second, Mark specifically mentions that Jesus touched the man out of compassion. One would be considered unclean if a person came into physical contact with someone with leprosy. Rather than Jesus becoming unclean, the unclean person is cleansed of his disease. Third, Jesus demonstrated that he was not opposed to the Law of Moses by instructing the man to present himself to the priest (who would pronounce him cured) and make an offering for his healing (cf. Lev. 13:47–14:54).

Living It Out

Two thoughts stand out for reflection in today's reading. First, ivory tower theologians are people who make theological pronouncements without any real-world ministry experience. They write and speak from a place of isolation. They deal in the theoretical. The same can be said of many Christians that isolate themselves from the hurts and troubles of people. One thing is clear in these stories; Jesus did not isolate himself from those he came to save.

Second, Jesus' need to pray is sometimes hard to understand since he is God. We should never forget, however, that he is also man. We learn from Jesus that he did not think he could do life effectively without prayer. In this passage, a major decision needed to be made—set up shop in Capernaum or leave a growing ministry to preach elsewhere. Immediately after finishing his time of prayer, he leaves Capernaum for a time. "Numerical success" didn't determine Jesus' decision but rather the Father's guidance in prayer. If praying for guidance was important for Jesus, how much more should it be for us!

Day Three

Blasphemy and Bad Company

Mark 2:1–17

The Big Picture

Today's reading is part of a larger section of material focused on conflict between Jesus and the religious establishment (Mark 2:1–3:6). The five conflict stories help the reader better understand why many of the religious leaders hated Jesus. Each episode is punctuated by a question (the first four are from Jesus' opponents): "Who can forgive sins but God alone?" (2:7); "Why does he eat with tax collectors and sinners?" (2:16); "Why do John's disciples and the Pharisees' disciples fast, but your disciples do not fast?" (2:18); "Look, why are they doing what is not lawful on the Sabbath?" (2:24). In the final story, Jesus asks the question, "Is it lawful to do good on the Sabbath or to do evil, to save life or to kill?" (3:4). The section culminates with the Pharisees and Herodians conspiring as to how they might kill Jesus (3:6).

Digging In

Jesus and his disciples return to Capernaum after their first tour of Galilee (2:1–12). As Jesus is teaching, the large crowd keeps any more people from being able to enter the house. A paralytic is brought to Jesus by four friends who refuse to be dissuaded by the size of the crowd. Since they cannot get him to Jesus through the front door, they take him to the roof, remove a portion of it, and lower him down before Jesus. Jesus sees the faith of the paralytic and the friends and pronounces the man's sins forgiven.

The scribes who witnessed the healing and the forgiving of the man's sins concluded that Jesus was guilty of blasphemy because only God has the prerogative to forgive sins. Mark wants the reader to understand that the scribes were right in understanding that the ability to forgive sins is a divine prerogative and therefore Jesus must be God. Jesus knows immediately what they are thinking and asks if it is easier to forgive sins or to heal a man. In one sense, saying someone's sins are forgiven is easier—how could you prove it since it is not visible and verifiable—but forgiveness requires a divine work to become real. Jesus heals the paralytic to substantiate the claim that "the Son of Man has authority on earth to forgive sins" (2:10). The man rises to his feet, and to the amazement of the crowd, takes his mat and leaves. The crowd responds appropriately by giving glory and praise to God.

Jesus refers to himself as the "Son of Man," which is Jesus' favorite self-designation. The background to the title is found in Daniel 7:13–14. The Son of Man is pictured as a heavenly figure that in the end times is entrusted by God with authority, glory, and power. Outside the four Gospels, Son of Man is used in the New Testament, only by Stephen (Acts 7:56) and John in Revelation 1:13; 14:14. Jesus used the term because most Jewish people did not understand it to be a reference to the Messiah.

Many think that the main point of this passage is to encourage evangelism by bringing people to Jesus. However, the passage is about Jesus' authority to forgive sin. Only God can forgive sin, and if Jesus demonstrates his authority to forgive sin by the healing of the paralytic, then the reasonable conclusion is that Jesus is divine.

In the second of the five conflict stories, Jesus calls Levi (Matthew) to be his disciple. Levi follows Jesus in discipleship just as the four fishermen did. Jesus is gathering around him an odd assortment of followers! The way Levi followed Jesus was by introducing his friends to Jesus, which is what being a fisher of men means. Evangelism is an important aspect of following Jesus.

Jesus is associating with an unlikely crowd—"tax collectors and sinners." These were the kind of people the Pharisees sought to avoid. The Pharisees were a strict sect within Judaism dedicated to living very devoted lives. They gave strict adherence to their oral traditions and would have considered association with seemingly irreligious people to have caused them to become spiritually unclean. They do not have the courage to ask Jesus directly, but instead ask his disciples why he associates with such people. To eat with someone was a sign of friendship.

Jesus responds by speaking a parable—comparing himself to a physician and the tax collectors and sinners as those who are sick. Jesus was speaking "tongue in cheek" when he implied that the Pharisees were not sick and did not need a physician. The truth is that a doctor can do very little for a sick person if they refuse to acknowledge their sickness. The point in this passage is that Jesus came to save sinners.

Living It Out

When one considers how to apply these verses, the larger context must be kept in mind. Mark has brought together a series of stories to help the reader understand why the religious establishment hated Jesus. We should not be surprised when we discover that the world we live in, hates him for many of the same reasons. The world may be willing to acknowledge Jesus as a good man, but to say Jesus is God and he has the authority to forgive sins is tantamount to religious intolerance in their minds. Saying that there are many ways to God is culturally acceptable. But, saying there is only one way to God is unforgivable. If we follow Jesus, we will find that the kind of opposition we will encounter is similar to the kind of opposition he faced.

Too often we fail to understand that an essential part of following Jesus is doing what Levi did—introducing family and friends to Jesus.

Jesus is the only one who can make an eternal difference in their lives. He has the authority to forgive sin! Levi demonstrates what it means to follow Jesus and to fish for people.

Controversies Continue

Mark 2:18–3:6

The Big Picture

Yesterday's reading revealed that the Pharisees accused Jesus of blasphemy for his forgiving the sins of the paralytic and his association with tax collectors and sinners. In today's reading, we examine the final three conflict stories. The first concerns the issue of fasting, and the last two concern the Sabbath day. The entire section (Mark 2:1–3:6) culminates with the Pharisees and Herodians plotting to kill Jesus (3:6).

Digging In

The third conflict story centers on the practice of fasting (2:18–22). The Law of Moses required only one day of fasting a year on the Day of Atonement (cf. Lev. 16:29, 31; 23:27–32). Four other yearly fasts were observed by the Jews after the Babylonian exile (Zech. 7:5; 8:19). In Jesus' day, the Pharisees fasted twice a week. Jesus was not opposed to fasting (Matt. 6:16) and the early church practiced the spiritual discipline as well (Acts 13:2).

Jesus responds to them with three brief parables. In the first, the inauguration of the kingdom is like a wedding feast, and no one attends a wedding feast while fasting. A Jewish wedding was a joyful occasion, and the celebration could last as long as a week. To fast during such festivities was unthinkable. Fasting was associated with times of sorrow and repentance. A day was coming, however, when Jesus, the bridegroom, would be taken from them by death, and then fasting would be appropriate.

The second and third parables are called twin parables because of their similarities and the fact that they teach the same lesson. You would not take a new piece of cloth and attach it to an old garment because when you washed it the new patch would shrink and pull away, ruining the old garment. In a similar way, you would not put fresh grape juice into an old wineskin. In ancient times, goat skins were used to hold wine. As the fresh grape juice fermented and the wine expanded, the old wineskin would lack flexibility and it would burst and the wine would be lost. Jesus brings a newness that cannot be confined within the old forms of religion.

The fourth conflict story is a debate between Jesus and the Pharisees over appropriate behavior on the Sabbath (Mark 2:23–28). Apparently, the Pharisees were keeping a close watch on Jesus and his disciples. The Pharisees were complaining that Jesus' disciples were harvesting on the Sabbath day. The Law forbids harvesting on the Sabbath (Exod. 34:21), protecting a farmer from greed and ignoring the worship of God. Furthermore, this law protected the laborers from being overworked and taken advantage of.

Jesus and the disciples were clearly not harvesting as a farmer would do. Instead, they were merely picking the grain to satisfy their hunger, which was entirely appropriate behavior according to Deuteronomy 23:25: "When you enter your neighbor's standing grain, you may pluck heads of grain with your hand, but do not put a sickle to your neighbor's grain."

Jesus appeals to the example of David in 1 Samuel 21:1–6. Each Sabbath, twelve fresh loaves of bread were to be set on a table in the holy place (Exod. 25:30; Lev. 24:5–9). The old loaves were eaten by the priest. The relationship between the Old Testament incident and in the apparent infringement of the Sabbath by the disciples lies in the fact that, on both occasions, godly men did something *seemingly* forbidden. What the disciples did was clearly appropriate. And since doing good and saving a life (even on the Sabbath) is always "lawful," both David and the disciples were within the spirit of the law (cf. Isa. 58:6–7).

Jewish oral traditions had so multiplied the requirements and restrictions for keeping the Sabbath that the day became a burden to God's people rather than a blessing. Jesus clearly stated that God intended the Sabbath for man, that is, for spiritual, mental, and physical renewal (Mark 2:27). Jesus concludes by declaring that he, the Son of Man, is Lord of the Sabbath. His point is that he has the authority to interpret the true meaning of the Sabbath and particularly to override the oral traditions of the Pharisees that made the day a burden.

The final conflict story also takes place on a Sabbath day (3:1–6). What makes this story different from the previous four is that Jesus asks the question and his opponents are unable to answer. This story connects to the previous story in the fact that Jesus demonstrates by his healing of the man with the withered hand that he truly is the Lord of the Sabbath.

Jesus put his opponents in a difficult position with the question he asks them (3:4). The irony is that while Jesus is preparing to heal a man, the Pharisees are considering how to put Jesus to death-clarifying who is guilty of breaking the Sabbath ("Is it lawful to do good on the Sabbath or to do evil, to save life or to kill?").

The Pharisees remain silent. After looking around at them, Jesus' emotions are mixed. He is righteously indignant at their callousness, but at the same time, he is grieved over their hardness of heart (3:5). Jesus commands the man to stretch out his hand, and as he does, his hand is restored. Rather than praising God for the man's healing, the Pharisees and Herodians conspire about how to kill Jesus.

Living It Out

The Pharisees raised their traditions to the level of Scripture (cf. 7:1–23). Before we criticize them too quickly, however, we must ask ourselves if there are not matters of preference with which we have done the same. Whether in worship styles, or the proper attire for church—casual or "Sunday best"—believers must make sure that their preferences or cultural traditions are not confused with Scripture.

An Expanding Ministry

Mark 3:7–19

The Big Picture

The second cycle of Jesus' ministry in Galilee (Mark 3:7–6:6a) repeats and expands on much of the same material found in the first cycle (1:14–3:6). The passage begins with a summary of Jesus' ministry (3:7–12; cf. 1:14–15), with an emphasis on his healing more than on his preaching this time. The cycle continues with Jesus' appointment of the Twelve (3:13–19; cf. 1:16–20) and a confrontation with the Pharisees (3:20–30; cf. 2:1–3:5)—a confrontation so great that the Pharisees charged Jesus with being empowered by Beelzebub. Rather than ending the second cycle at this point, however, Mark shows Jesus turning to the crowds with his message (3:31–4:34). The cycle continues on with the narration of a series of mighty miracles and a rejection of Jesus by his hometown of Nazareth (4:35–6:6a).

Digging In

In the opening verses, Mark continues to emphasize Jesus' increasing popularity and expanding influence (3:7–12). His point is to highlight the difference of opinion between what the crowds think about Jesus and what the religious establishment thinks about him. People travel from near and far in response to the spreading news about him. He instructs his disciples to keep a boat ready because the crowds are pressing in on him. Mark continues to emphasize the cosmic nature of Jesus' ministry by his reference to unclean spirits.

Jesus' appointment of the Twelve marks a significant advancement in his ministry (3:13–19). Jesus' philosophy of ministry focused heavily on discipleship. He ministered to the crowds, but out of the crowd he chooses twelve. The number twelve was symbolic of the twelve tribes of Israel. Jesus is establishing a new people of God. The New Testament contains four lists of the twelve apostles (Matt. 10:2–4; Luke 6:13–16; Acts 1:13).

When you compare the lists, you discover that Peter is always first and Judas Iscariot is always last, Philip is always fifth, and James the Son of Alphaeus is always ninth. It is at least possible that Jesus divided the Twelve into three groups of four. The reason for the differences in a few of the names among the various lists is due to the fact that many of them had two names (i.e., Matthew/Levi; Simon/Peter). Luke mentions that Jesus chose the Twelve only after he had spent the night in prayer (Luke 6:12).

Jesus' method of discipleship is seen in the fact that he called them "to be with him." As they spent time traveling together, he was able to teach them privately. While traveling with him, they got firsthand experience in ministry. Jesus' method of discipleship enabled him to multiply his ministry by sending them out to preach and giving them authority "to drive out demons" (3:14–15).

The twelve disciples should not be thought of in an idealized sort of way. They were rather ordinary men in many ways, and some of them were very rough around the edges. They were characterized, however, as having hearts for God and a willingness to follow Jesus even when the religious establishment rejected him. When we look at these men, and the many other men and women who were Jesus' followers, we find that they are not much different from you or me. What is evident is that Jesus transformed their lives, and he can transform ours as well.

Simon Peter was a partner in a successful fishing business. He became the leading spokesperson for the group. His brother Andrew lived in the shadow of his more famous brother; however, he was responsible for introducing his brother to Jesus (John 1:40–42). James and John were both sons of Zebedee. They had a fiery temper and were nicknamed "sons of Thunder." James was the first of the apostles martyred (Acts 12:2), and John would eventually be exiled to Patmos (Rev. 1:9).

While Philip was not a part of the inner circle, he is listed fifth in each of the four lists of apostles. He is mentioned in numerous passages and responded to Jesus when he was called to follow (John 1:43). Bartholomew is probably the same individual called Nathaniel in John 1:43–51. If so, he was known for his outspoken honesty. Thomas is most famous for doubting the resurrection of Jesus in John 20:24–29; however, it should not be forgotten that his declaration of Jesus' deity is one of the highest in the New Testament: "my Lord and my God" (John 20:28). Matthew (Levi the tax collector) would have formerly been thought of as a traitor by his own people. The power of Jesus is seen in the fact that his gospel stands first in our New Testament canon. James, the son of Alphaeus, was never given much recognition in the four Gospels. Thaddeus, also known as Judas son of James, is sometimes confused with Judas Iscariot. Not much is known about him from the Gospels. Simon the Zealot may very well have been a political revolutionary before he met Jesus. If so, he was transformed by the power of God and ceased seeking to establish God's kingdom by a militaristic force. Finally, Judas Iscariot is listed last in all four lists for a good reason. Apparently, he betrayed Jesus (in part) out of a love of money. He reminds us how close one can be to Jesus yet fall short of saving faith.

Living It Out

We are amazed at how widely the word of Jesus' ministry spread by word of mouth. As Jesus preached, cast out demons, and healed the sick, people from ever-expanding distances were drawn to him. While churches today search for greater and more effective ways to use technology—which is not necessarily bad—people are drawn by the Spirit of God to churches where ministry is done by God's Spirit and for Christ's glory.

We should also not miss from today's reading how very important discipleship was in the ministry of Jesus. The first act of ministry after Jesus was tempted was to call four fishermen to follow him. He then called a tax collector to follow him. Eventually, he called twelve to be his disciples. He ministered to the crowds but focused on the Twelve. These were not the most impressive men in the world's eyes, but they were passionate for God and loved Jesus. If a church is going to reach its community for Christ, the church must have a strategy for discipleship.

Family, Accusations, and Followers

Mark 3:20–35

The Big Picture

This passage parallels the opposition Jesus encountered earlier in Mark 2:1–3:6. Here, the opposition is intensified as his family believes Jesus to be "out of his mind" (3:21). The religious leaders believe Jesus casts out demons by the power of Beelzebub, the prince of demons. In contrast, Jesus' true family members are those who listen to his Word and obey it.

This passage is the first example of a literary device popularly known as a "Markan sandwich," in which one story is placed within another so that the two interpret each other and follows an A/B/A pattern. Here, Mark begins telling us about the family of Jesus, interrupts this story by telling us about Jesus' confrontation with the scribes, and then returns to the story of Jesus' family.

As mentioned above, we have three groups in this passage: First, Jesus' family misunderstands him and seeks to take custody of him. Second, there are Jesus' critics, who accuse him of being a sorcerer aligned with Satan. Third, there are those who are seated around Jesus, seeking to live in obedience to his Word. These he describes as his true family.

Digging In

The crowds continue to follow Jesus as he and the disciples do not even have time to eat (3:20). His family sets out to take control of him because they think he is "out of his mind" (3:21). They obviously were concerned about both his physical and mental well-being. Interestingly enough, his family drops out of the story until after Jesus' encounter with the scribes from Jerusalem. The fact that Jesus' family doubted him must have been very hurtful to Jesus (cf. John 7:5).

The central section of the passage describes Jesus as being accused of casting out demons by the power of Beelzebul, the prince of demons (3:22). The fact that the scribes (teachers of the law) came from Jerusalem suggests they were there in an official capacity. Beelzebul was another name for Satan. No one could doubt Jesus' authority to cast out demons, so the scribes challenge the source of his power. Jesus' first response is to point out the absurdity of the accusation. If Satan is empowering him to cast out demons, then Satan is fighting against himself and his own kingdom (3:23–26). Satan would be engaging in a civil war and Satan's kingdom would self-destruct.

If Jesus is not empowered by Satan, and is casting out Satan's demons, then he is stronger than Satan. Jesus brings this point out in a brief parable in verse 27. In this parable, the strongman must be Satan, the house would be the person indwelt by a demon, and the one who plunders the strongman's house is Jesus, who casts the demon out, setting the person free. Jesus' exorcisms are an example of tying up the strongman and setting people free from demonic control. The background may be found in Isaiah 49:24–25, where God the divine warrior defeats Israel's enemies and takes "plunder" for his people.

Jesus then warns the scribes that they are in danger of committing an "eternal sin" (3:28–30). These verses have been very troubling to believers throughout history. We must look at what Jesus says closely in order to understand exactly what he is and is not saying when he speaks of "blasphemies against the Holy Spirit." While Jesus' opponents accuse him of casting out demons by the power of Satan, he warns them about committing the "unpardonable sin." Mark records Jesus' first use of the phrase, "Truly, I say to you,"[4] which is used to introduce an authoritative statement or assertion by Jesus.

Jesus' statement highlights both God's mercy and judgment. God's mercy is demonstrated in the wideness of God's willingness to forgive sins of all kinds (3:28). God's judgment is seen in the statement that "whoever blasphemes against the Holy Spirit never has forgiveness, but is guilty of an eternal sin" (3:29). The blasphemous statement made by the scribes was that Jesus' miracles, especially his exorcisms, were the result of an unclean spirit (demon). Mark identifies this particular blasphemy as being unforgivable. This blasphemy reflects a settled disposition and rejection of the evident work of God in Christ by those (the scribes) who knew God's Word better than any other people in the world. By their definitive rejection of the work of the Spirit in the person of Christ, they cut themselves off from the grace of God in Christ. The scribes kept saying "he has an unclean spirit." Obviously, those who are saved by Christ and those who fear committing that sin have not committed it.

At this point, Jesus' "mother and brothers" return to the story (3:31–35). A list of Jesus' brothers appears in Mark 6:3 and Matthew 13:55 (both also mention "his sisters" [Matt. 13:56]). The absence of Joseph may suggest that he has already died. The fact that Mark describes them as "standing outside" may imply that at this time his family is outside the circle of his followers. However, after Jesus' resurrection, his family appears to have become his followers (1 Cor. 15:7).

Jesus' statement is not intended to demean the importance of our earthly family, which is taught throughout the Bible. Instead, he highlights the appearance of a new family, the people of God—the church. Jesus' new family seeks to live life in a way pleasing to him demonstrated by repentance, faith, and discipleship. To be a disciple of Jesus is to be a doer of his Word and not merely a hearer (James 1:22–25).

Living It Out

There are several insights we should glean from today's reading. First, we should never be surprised when others oppose us as followers of Jesus. Sometimes those who oppose us may even be those who love us. Our first allegiance, however, is to follow King Jesus. At other times, we may experience rejection by the world, as Jesus warned us in John 15:18–16:4. A second thought is that Jesus sees the church as his family. How encouraging to know that God is our Father and Christ Jesus our Lord is our elder brother!

Kingdom Parables

Mark 4:1–20

The Big Picture

Yesterday's reading was a striking reminder that Jesus faced significant opposition from both the religious establishment and even his own family. The question is why did he face such opposition? The point of Mark 4:1–34 is that the opposition was not because of the messenger, or the message, but the unreceptive hearts of many of his hearers.

The parable discourse (4:1–34), along with chapter 13, are the two major teaching passages in Mark. The parables of chapter 4 interpret the events in chapters 1 through 3. These "kingdom parables" describe the implications of the arrival of the kingdom of God. Parables can be a simple narrative analogy, simile, metaphor, comparison, or allegory intended to make a spiritual point(s). The parable discourse consists of an introduction (4:1–2) and a conclusion (4:33–34) framing five parables, with the parable of the soils being the key parable for understanding what is taking place in Jesus' ministry.

Digging In

Once again, Mark emphasizes Jesus teaching large crowds by the Sea of Galilee. He gets into a boat to provide a little separation from the crowd. He calls on the crowd to listen as he teaches them. This collection of parables begins with the longest parable (4:3–9), and its interpretation (4:13–20) focuses on various types of soil as an analogy for various conditions of the human heart. In between the parable and Jesus' interpretation, Jesus explains to the disciples why he speaks to the crowds in parables (4:10–12).

The parable of the soils accurately depicts the way that farming was often done in the ancient world—the seed was sown before the soil was fully prepared. Normally, though not always, the plowing followed the spreading of the seed. Sometimes seed was sown on the fringes of the field, on roadways alongside the field. Some seed would fall in sections where the soil was very shallow and other seed where the soil was cluttered with weeds and briars. The goal, however, was for the seed to fall on the good soil where there would be a harvest.

The scene changes, and Jesus is alone with his disciples explaining why he teaches the crowds in parables (4:10–12). The disciples' question concerns all the parables and not just this one. Jesus' genuine followers are permitted to understand the secret (literally mystery) of the kingdom of God—namely, that the kingdom of God has come (1:14–15) and Christ the Son of God is in their midst (1:1). First-century Jews mistakenly believed that the kingdom of God would be fully inaugurated with the coming of the Messiah. However, the kingdom will not be consummated until the second coming of Jesus.

Jesus' reply to the disciples' question suggests that the parables were intended to prevent outsiders from understanding them, so that they would be unable to repent and be forgiven. The quotation from Isaiah 6:9–10 implies that this was an intentional judgment on the hearers. Jesus' teaching in parables and the resulting unbelief of outsiders fulfilled what the Scriptures had predicted.

The parable of the soils, however, indicates that the hearers had a part to play in their rejection as well. The hardness, shallowness, and cluttering of their hearts worked against the Word taking root in them.

While the parable focuses on man's responsibility in responding to the message, Jesus' explanation focuses on God's sovereignty in the process. Jesus rebukes the disciples for their failure to comprehend the parable of the soils. Even Jesus' disciples need help to understand the parables (4:13). Jesus' interpretation of the parable of the soils is straightforward (4:13–20). The hard soil represents a hardhearted person. Consistent rejection of God's Word hardens a person's heart. As Jesus makes clear, a cosmic element is involved, since Satan comes and takes away the Word sown in the heart of the hardhearted person. The shallow soil represents a person who makes a shallow and emotional response to the Word. The evidence of this response is when persecution comes because of the Word they supposedly received, they fall away just as quickly as they initially responded to the Word.

The seed sown among the thorns depicts the Word beginning to work but is choked out by the worldliness of the person's life. John the apostle made a similar warning when he told his readers: "Do not love the world or the things in the world. If anyone loves the world, the love of the Father is not in him. For everything in the world—the lust of the flesh, the lust of the eyes, and the pride in one's possessions—is not from the Father, but is from the world" (1 John 2:15–16). The good soil is represented by those seated around Jesus at the end of the previous chapter. They hear the Word and become doers of it. Their lives bear fruit-giving evidence of their commitment to Jesus.

Living It Out

The key question is: Which kind of soil are you? The Spirit and Word work together to bring people to Christ. The Spirit uses the Word to bring conviction to a person's heart. James notes the importance of the Word in the new birth: "By his own choice, he gave us birth by the word of truth so that we would be a kind of first fruits of his creatures" (James 1:18). Peter makes a similar point: "You have been born again—not of perishable seed but of imperishable—through the living and enduring word of God" (1 Pet. 1:23). As believers, we must be doers of the Word and not merely hearers. We must read and meditate on the Word and then put the Word into practice.

More Kingdom Parables

Mark 4:21–34

The Big Picture

The main thought in the remaining parables, as the discourse continues, is the centrality of hearing, obeying, and sharing the message of the kingdom (Mark 4:21–34). The miracles to follow demonstrate the power of Jesus' words as he "speaks" to nature, demons, sickness, and death, and they immediately respond. How can one fail to hear and obey him when he speaks? These ideas are brought out first in the brief parables of the lamp and the measure (4:21–25) and secondly in two seed parables (4:26–32). The phrase "ears to hear" in verse 23 repeats verse 9 and suggests once again that the only viable response to Jesus' teaching is to hear and obey.

Digging In

Jesus now compares the kingdom to a lamp. In the first century, a lamp was a small oil-burning clay vessel, intended to illuminate a room.

Jesus' point is that the message of the kingdom must not be hidden or extinguished. The purpose of a lamp is to bring light into a dark place and the same is true of the message of the kingdom. While the message of the kingdom was not fully revealed before the coming of Jesus, it is now made fully known. Those with ears to hear must pay careful attention to this kingdom message.

Once again Jesus calls on his listeners to pay close attention to what he is saying: "If anyone has ears to hear, let him listen." And he said to them, "Pay attention to what you hear" (4:24). The emphasis on hearing to comprehend cannot be missed. The parable of the measure comes from the practice of using a scoop to measure out grain to be sold in the market. Jesus' point is that we will receive back from God to the degree that we listen to God's Word and obey it. Note the divine passive "will be measured." This means that when we pay careful attention to Jesus' teaching, we will be rewarded by God. True "hearing" is not merely comprehending God's Word but involves putting God's Word into practice. Jesus' harshest opponents knew God's Word, but it had not transformed their lives. They thought they were what they knew. They were self-deluded.

Jesus explains that as a result of God's grace the reward will exceed one's effort. The idea of reciprocity should not be understood along the lines of the "health wealth" gospel. God will graciously give those who hear and obey even greater understanding of his Word, which is a tremendous incentive to reading, meditating on, and obeying God's Word. Those who refuse to open their hearts to kingdom truths will lose even what little understanding and blessing they may have originally possessed.

In many ways, this parable is comparable to the three soils from yesterday's reading. The parable would have been readily understood in an agrarian society (4:26–29). The parable's purpose is to give insight into the kingdom of God. The parable describes a farmer who does all that he can do—he scatters his seed. No blame should be attributed to the farmer for sleeping. The point is that there is only so much a farmer can do, and then he is dependent on God as seen in the detailed description of the growth of the seed, "The soil produces a crop by itself—first the blade, then the head, and then the full grain on the head" (4:28). The same point is true of the message of the kingdom. All gospel farmers can do is to sow the gospel-seed of the kingdom and then pray and wait expectantly to see what God does.

The parable of the mustard seed is a fitting conclusion to the parable discourse and is another picture of the kingdom of God. Once again, there is a seed sown; this time the seed sown is a small mustard seed. The point is that from this very tiny seed comes a plant with branches large enough for birds to nest in it. So, the kingdom of God, from a very small beginning—a Galilean carpenter and a small group of disciples—will become all-encompassing.[5] Mark indicates that these parables are representative of many more parables Jesus spoke. The disciples, however, were given further insight that the crowds were not privy to receiving.

Living It Out

The passage highlights three key truths. The first is that the kingdom inaugurated by Jesus' coming, remained something of a mystery until it was fully revealed in Jesus (cf. Eph. 3:2–6). What the Old Testament prophets pointed toward God was brought into full light with the arrival of Jesus. A second insight is that God's people are responsible for hearing, obeying, and sharing God's kingdom message. As James 1:22–25 says, being a "hearer only" is not enough. We must put into practice what we hear and then share it with those in darkness. The message of the kingdom is not to be hidden under a bed but placed on a lampstand to illuminate the darkness of this world. Finally, we are taught that the growth of the kingdom is in the hands of God, and there are no better hands for it to be in than God's.

Kingdom Authority over Nature and Demons

Mark 4:35–5:20

The Big Picture

Today's and tomorrow's readings recount Jesus' authority over nature, demons, sickness, and even death. The authority of Jesus' words (Mark 4:1–34) are confirmed by the authority of his deeds (4:35–5:43). Mark records four powerful acts by Jesus: he calms a storm, demonstrating his authority over nature; he casts a legion of demons out of a demonized man, demonstrating his authority over evil; and then in a "Markan sandwich," he heals a very sick woman and resuscitates a dead girl, thereby demonstrating his authority over sickness and death.

Digging In

After Jesus finished teaching the crowds, he and the disciples get into a boat to go across the Sea of Galilee. The Sea of Galilee is surrounded by high hills, which commonly funnel high winds onto the water creating large waves. The lake is approximately 700 feet below sea level but is deep enough that quite a large amount of water can be stirred up in a storm. The waves were beginning to fill the boat threatening their very survival (4:37).

The fact that Jesus is sleeping reveals his true humanity. Jesus was fully human and fully divine. We often emphasize his deity to the expense of his humanity. He apparently was exhausted from his day of teaching. The disciples' response is a common reaction when we find ourselves in trying situations. They interpret Jesus' sleep as a lack of concern for them. How could he sleep when they are in such danger? "Doesn't he care about us?" Notice they call Jesus "teacher" rather than Lord.

Jesus rebukes the wind using the same term he used to silence the demon in chapter 1. We shouldn't, however, interpret his use of the same term to mean that the storm was the result of demonic activity. Jesus is addressing the wind and the waves as a living entity to demonstrate his complete control over all such forces.

The disciples' excessive fear is a sign of a weak faith (cf. 5:15, 36; 6:50; 10:32; 16:8). God allows us, like he did with the disciples, to be put in circumstances where we are forced to trust in him so that our faith grows and matures. The climax of the passage however focuses not on the disciple's lack of faith but on Jesus' true identity. The disciples ask the question, "Who then is this? Even the wind and the sea obey him!" The most important question in all of life is: "Who do you believe Jesus to be?" Mark wants his readers to ask the same question. We know from our earlier studies that he is the long-awaited Messiah and the Son of God. Mark answers the disciples' question in the next passage.

The story of the Gadarene demoniac seems bizarre to twenty-first century readers because while we believe in the devil, intellectually, we don't believe in him theologically. The passage teaches clearly that a cosmic conflict between the kingdom of God and the kingdom of darkness is taking place in our world (read 2 Cor. 4:4; Eph. 6:10–12).

As the passage unfolds, the depth of depravity into which a person can sink becomes clear (5:1–5). The event takes place in Gentile territory. Mark describes an individual who is clearly demonized. He has no concern for personal dignity, lives in isolation, has supernatural strength, and his speech is controlled by the demon(s). Satan is a malicious, cruel, and powerful being.

Verses 6–13 reveal Jesus' absolute authority over the forces of evil. When the demon sees Jesus, it causes the man to run and bow down at Jesus' feet. The demon knows Jesus' true identity and confesses him as "the Son of the Most High God." The cowardly demon fears Jesus will torment him.

This passage is the only time in the gospels that Jesus engages a demon in conversation, possibly because it is the worst case of demonization he encountered. The demon referred to himself and those with it by the name "Legion." A Roman legion had six thousand soldiers. The demon asks for permission to go into a nearby herd of pigs rather than being sent out of the region. Jesus granted them permission, and approximately two thousand pigs stampeded into the Sea of Galilee. The disciples may have wished that they were back in the storm at sea!

The passage concludes by describing the wonderful change Jesus makes in the man's life (5:14–20). In verses 14–16, Mark contrasts the striking difference between the townspeople who beg Jesus to leave and the man set free who begs to be permitted to accompany Jesus. The changes in the man are phenomenal. Jesus tells the man to share with his family what great things God had done for him. He immediately begins to report broadly what great things Jesus had done for him.

Living It Out

We conclude today's reading with a couple of final thoughts. The first passage ends with an important question: "Who is this man?" In the Old Testament, Yahweh alone commands the storms. God is the one who controls the seas. Psalm 65:7 reads, "You silence the roar of the seas, the roar of their waves, and the tumult of the nations." Psalm 89:9 reads, "You rule the raging sea; when its waves surge, you still them." Psalm 107:28–29 says, "Then they cried out to the LORD in their trouble, and he brought them out of their distress. He stilled the storm to a whisper, and the waves of the sea were hushed." Jesus Christ can do that which only God can do.

In light of the second story, we must be aware that we are in a cosmic war. We may be confident in our own salvation but feel a sense of hopelessness for the possibility of salvation for a friend or loved one. The story of the Gadarene demoniac should encourage us that there is no one outside the reach of God's transforming grace! If Jesus can set a man free from a legion of demons by his spoken word, then he can do the same for those for whom we pray! Never give up on someone!

Desperation and Faith

Mark 5:21–43

The Big Picture

Having read yesterday about Jesus' authority over nature and evil, today's reading focuses on Jesus' authority over sickness and death. These two stories are deliberately interwoven ("Markan sandwich"). The passage unfolds in three stages: a father's desperate plea for Jesus to heal his dying daughter (Mark 5:21–24) is interrupted by a very sick woman who demonstrates a very determined faith (5:25–34), and finally, the passage returns to the dying daughter (5:35–43). Mark heightens the suspense of what will happen to the dying girl by separating the beginning and ending of the story with the healing of the unnamed woman.

Digging In

Jesus returns to Galilee, and the crowds continue to flock to him. Jairus, a synagogue ruler, falls at Jesus' feet, begging him to come and heal his daughter before she dies. We learn that she is his only daughter and is twelve years of age. A synagogue ruler was responsible for overseeing synagogue services, selecting participants, maintaining order, and having some responsibilities for the building. The ruler was a layman and would have been very highly regarded in the community. No one, no matter how respected, is exempt from heartache. His request is a picture of desperation, dependence, and urgency. One can scarcely imagine what each passing moment did to Jairus's soul as the crowds made movement difficult for them.

Suddenly, the scene changes dramatically as an unnamed woman with a determined faith enters the picture. Interestingly enough, while we know Jairus's name, this woman remains unnamed.

Mark graphically describes her condition and the extent of her suffering (5:25–26). She is physically sick, emotionally broken, and financially destitute. Her physical condition rendered her ceremonially unclean, but the woman believes if she can touch Jesus' garment she could be made well. The fact that she entered into the crowd, while being considered ritually unclean, demonstrated both her courage and faith. When she touched Jesus' garment, she knew immediately that she was healed. At the same time, Jesus was aware that power had departed from him.

Faith was alive in her, but all others saw when they looked at her was a disgusting sickness that brought her character into question. In the ancient world, many believed that one's sickness was the result of their sin. Jesus once encountered a blind man, and his disciples asked, "Rabbi, who sinned, this man or his parents, that he was born blind?" (John 9:2). This woman suffered with a bleeding uterus, and with a sickness like that, one can only imagine the kind of sin she committed. Their thinking could not have been any more wrong.

At this very important moment in Jairus's daughter's life, Jesus stops to draw attention to this woman (5:33–34). His interaction with her announces to all that she is a woman of faith and she is healed. After twelve long years, she is healed! Note that just as Jairus fell at Jesus' feet so did this desperate woman. Jesus calls her daughter a tender term of address. The Greek word for "saved" is the same for "healed." Here, both physical healing ("healed from your affliction") and spiritual healing ("go in peace") are brought together.

At this moment, Jairus receives the worst possible news—his daughter is dead (5:35). There is nothing more that can be done. Up to this point in the gospel, Jesus has not brought anyone back from the dead. The remainder of the passage is punctuated by three statements from Jesus. The first is a word of hope: "Don't be afraid. Only believe" (5:36; cf. 4:40). Jesus has just told the unnamed woman, "Your faith has saved you." Now he tells Jairus, "Believe in me!" Faith crushes fear!

Jesus takes along his inner circle (Peter, James, and John) along with Jairus and finds a gathering already assembled. For the first time in Mark, these three disciples are singled out from the rest. Jesus asserts that the child is not dead but asleep, which is a word of revelation (5:39). He can restore life as easily as one can be awakened from sleep. What is disturbing is how quickly the crowd's tears turn to laughter and derision.

Finally, Jesus speaks a word of resurrection power (5:41). Accompanied only by the three disciples and the little girl's parents, Jesus stands over her little dead body and says, "Talitha koum" (which is translated, "Little girl, I say to you, get up"). The event made such a deep impression on those present that, when it was told, Jesus' Aramaic words were recounted. Mark translated them for his Greek-speaking audience.

Living It Out

The importance of faith is highlighted in this passage (cf. 4:40). Both Jairus and this woman demonstrated desperation and faith. The woman had to wait twelve years to be healed, and Jairus had to experience the death of his daughter. We don't know why the woman had to wait so long to be healed or why Jesus didn't immediately heal the dying girl. True faith trusts in God's power and timing.

What do we do when he doesn't heal? We must trust him and believe that God has another plan for our lives. Seldom did he raise people from the dead, and he left many unhealed. We must trust him when he heals and trust him when he doesn't heal. His intention is not to make us comfortable but holy!

Finally, although hundreds were crowded around as Jesus made his way to Jairus's home, only two people experienced his power. Remaining untouched by Jesus' power is possible while being in Jesus' presence. Never forget that desperation and faith drive a person to the feet of the Galilean carpenter, and that is where you experience his power!

Penetrating the Darkness

Mark 6:1–29

The Big Picture

In the passage we study today, Jesus and John the Baptist are described as taking the gospel to hard places. The passage can be divided into three sections. The first is a tragic encounter between Jesus and his friends in Nazareth (Mark 6:1–6). In the second, Jesus sends his disciples out on a short-term mission trip (6:7–13). The final section describes the brutal execution of John the Baptist (6:14–29).

Digging In

Jesus returns home to Nazareth, which was about twenty miles southwest of Capernaum. Jesus already had some difficult moments with his family (cf. 3:19–21, 31–34). These encounters must have been very painful for him. Nevertheless, he returns home to minister and serve the people of Nazareth. The crowd is amazed initially by Jesus' words. Yet, in the next moment, they begin to ask him hostile questions. At the conclusion of these six questions, they are described as taking offense at him (6:2–3).

Jesus responds to their questions with both a proverb and amazement. The main point of the proverb is that the people of Nazareth were incapable of appreciating who he truly was because they identified themselves so closely to him. Familiarity has a way of breeding contempt. Mark next evaluates Jesus' visit (6:5–6). The idea is not that Jesus was incapable of performing any miracles, because he did heal a few sick people, but he chose not to do many miracles there because of their lack of faith. The Gospels refer to Jesus being "amazed" only two times—here at unbelief and the other time at the faith of a centurion (Matt. 8:10).

Jesus was obviously not deterred by this opposition because he sends his disciples out as his representatives (6:7–13). He empowers them for ministry. Because they will face satanic opposition, he gives them authority over unclean spirits. The purpose of going two-by-two is to bolster credibility (confirming a fact by two witnesses) and provide mutual encouragement and support. Jesus limited what they could take on the journey so they could learn to trust in God's providential care. They should be prepared to encounter both acceptance and rejection. They healed the sick, cast out demons, and called people to repentance. Repentance is not about trying harder but instead confessing one's sin and turning to Jesus in faith.

The next passage describes the execution of John the Baptist— quite the opposite of what the disciples just experienced (6:14–29)! Of all the gospel writers, Mark alone tells this sad story in such detail. King Herod (Antipas) was one of Herod the Great's sons. He heard reports of all that had been taking place through Jesus and his disciples. Speculation about Jesus' identity was swirling. Some even thought he might be John the Baptist raised from the dead.

Antipas had John the Baptist thrown into prison because John condemned him for taking his brother's wife, Herodias. Herodias was embittered toward John for the prophet's condemnation of their sinful relationship. Strangely enough, Antipas feared John and protected him from the clutches of his embittered wife. He knew John to be a godly man and a powerful preacher.

What an astonishing thought—a prophet of God, armed only with God's Word and the power of God's Spirit, unsettles the conscience of a powerful man. Antipas didn't fear people, but he feared this godly prophet. However, the one thing he refused to do was repent from his adulteress relationship with his brother's wife. Jesus once asked the question, "What can anyone give in exchange for his life?" (8:37). Antipas exchanged his soul for sexual pleasure.

Herodias, however, got the opportunity she wanted at Herod's birthday party. Antipas made the foolish statement to his stepdaughter, after she danced seductively for the gathering, that he would give her anything she wanted up to half his kingdom. At the instigation of her mother, she asks for the head of John the Baptist. Reluctantly, Antipas had John's head given to her on a platter. One can only imagine the hideous glee Herodias experienced when she saw John's bloody severed head.

When John's disciples learned of his execution, they took his corpse and placed it in a tomb. John was Jesus' forerunner in life and in death. The word *tomb* does not appear many times in Mark's Gospel. Tomb was used twice in the story about the Gadarene demoniac (5:3, 5). But we don't see it again, after this passage, until Jesus' corpse is placed in a tomb (15:46). John's body decomposed in his tomb, but the body of Jesus would not.

Living It Out

We focus our final thoughts on this larger passage on the execution of John the Baptist. Mark makes it clear that God's people should not look for their reward in this life. **After years of faithful service, John's final days were spent in prison culminating in a violent decapitation.** Like Stephen, murdered by a mob in Jerusalem; James, executed under Herod Agrippa I; and others, of whom the world is not worthy, he was called to seal his commitment to Christ with his own blood.

Stories like these are a clear reminder that our best days are yet to come, on the other side of the grave. Here, in this world, we must walk by faith, and not by sight. And, if we look for man's praise and earthly riches, we will be greatly disappointed. Maybe no one ever

understood this fact better than the apostle Paul who wrote the following words: "For I consider that the sufferings of this present time
are not worth comparing with the glory that is going to be revealed to
us" (Rom. 8:18).

God of the Impossible

Mark 6:30–56

The Big Picture

In today's reading, we examine two of Jesus' most famous miracles: the feeding of the 5,000 (Mark 6:30–44) and his walking on water (6:45–56). Many people do not believe that miracles really took place in Jesus' ministry, but it is undeniable that the Bible presents Jesus as a worker of miracles and the historical evidence supporting those claims is overwhelming. The prophet Jeremiah wrote: "Ah Lord GOD! You yourself made the heavens and earth by your great power and with your outstretched arm. Nothing is too difficult for you!" (Jer. 32:17). Later, in the same chapter, God confirms Jeremiah's words, when he says: "Look, I am the LORD, the God over every creature. Is anything too difficult for me?" (Jer. 32:27). The one who spoke into existence all things is more than able to feed thousands with a few pieces of bread and a couple of fish and to walk on the water (John 1:1–3).

Digging In

After describing the execution of John the Baptist, Mark recounts the return of the Twelve and need for a time of rest and refreshment.

However, refreshment was extremely difficult for Jesus and his disciples due to the large crowds. Mark shows both the relentless pursuit of the crowds and Jesus' compassionate heart toward them. The reason for Jesus' compassion was that he knew they were like sheep without a shepherd. People are not an inconvenience to Jesus, but instead, are the reason for his coming.

Jesus demonstrates himself as a compassionate shepherd by teaching the people. A shepherd was not an easy profession in the ancient (or modern!) world. A shepherd had to walk great distances, fight off wild animals, search for sheep that wandered away, and sometimes carry them back to the flock on his shoulders. There was seldom enough to eat and never enough time to sleep.

In both the Old and New Testaments, the leaders of God's people are referred to as shepherds. However, they often cared more about themselves than God's people. Ezekiel 34:2–6 is one of the most famous passages on the failure of Israel's leaders/shepherds to care for their flock.

> Son of man, prophesy against the shepherds of Israel. Prophesy, and say to them, "This is what the Lord GOD says to the shepherds: Woe to the shepherds of Israel, who have been feeding themselves! Shouldn't the shepherds feed their flock? You eat the fat, wear the wool, and butcher the fattened animals, but you do not tend the flock. For you have not strengthened the weak, healed the sick, bandaged the injured, brought back the strays, or sought the lost. Instead, you have ruled them with violence and cruelty. They were scattered for lack of a shepherd; they became food for all the wild animals when they were scattered. My flock went astray on all the mountains and every high hill. My flock was scattered over the whole face of the earth, and there was no one searching or seeking for them."

At the end of the day, the disciples were faced with a seemingly impossible situation. The evident problem was there was no way, in such a desolate location, to get enough food together to feed the enormous crowd. The disciples' ingenious recommendation was to send them away! They looked at the situation from their limited human perspective. All these weary disciples could see was a swelling sea of hungry humanity. From Jesus' perspective, the crowds were not an infringement but an opportunity. Great opportunities are often disguised as unsolvable problems!

Jesus puts the disciples to the test. He wants to stretch their faith. They only see the odds against them and fail to see the Savior who stands before them. Like the disciples, we shouldn't try and determine what is and is not possible for God. God does some of his greatest work in our most impossible situations. While the disciples looked to their own resources, Jesus turned his eyes toward heaven.

Jesus instructs that the crowd be placed in groups of hundreds and fifties so the food could be easily distributed. After praying, the disciples distribute the fish and the bread until everyone is full. After everyone had all they wanted to eat, there were twelve baskets full of leftovers, one for each of the disciples. Mark indicates that there were approximately five thousand men, which does not seem to include women and children. This feeding miracle is normally called "the feeding of the five thousand," but many more were present.

The second miracle in today's reading is Jesus walking on the water (Mark 6:45–52). Apparently, the disciples may have been a little resistant to leave, for Jesus "made them get into the boat." After forcing them into the boat, he launched them out into the sea. After Jesus sends the disciples away, he goes to the mountain to pray, which is the second time in Mark's Gospel Jesus is described as praying (cf. 1:35). Both times of prayer followed significant ministry success. After the feeding of the five thousand, John says the people wanted to force him to become king (John 6:14–15).

Late into the night the disciples find themselves struggling against a strong head wind. Jesus is not unaware of their situation and in the early morning hours, sometime between 3 to 6 a.m., he comes to them walking on the water. The last thing the disciples expected to see in those early morning hours was Jesus walking on the water! They were terrified, thinking they were seeing a ghost.

Mark makes the odd statement that Jesus "wanted to pass by them." These words have been understood in a variety of ways. The best understanding is rooted in the Old Testament idea of a theophany, an appearance and manifestation of God to his people. Two passages that add some insight to the meaning of the situation are Exodus 33:18–23 and 1 Kings 19:11. The latter passage reads:

> Then he said, "Go out and stand on the mountain in the LORD's presence." At that moment, the LORD passed by!

The disciples respond in fear, but Jesus speaks words of assurance and enters the boat. He calms their fears by identifying himself: "It is I. Don't be afraid." Jesus' words recall the name God revealed to Moses at the burning bush (Exod. 3:14).

Jesus walking on the sea is a powerful demonstration of his sovereignty over the world he created. The Old Testament teaches that God alone rules over the seas (Ps. 107:28–30). The disciples failed to grasp the significance of the moment. If they had understood the feeding, they would not have been amazed at his walking on the water.

The final verses in this chapter are another reminder of the endless needs of people and Jesus' compassion in taking time for people (6:53–56). Gennesaret was the fertile plain on the northwest side of the lake. These verses reveal several important thoughts about Jesus' ministry. We see the geographical extent of Jesus' ministry and that his ministry extended to all kinds of people. Those who believed in him needed only to touch the fringe of his garments. The reference to "the end of his robe" refers to the tassels worn by Jewish men on their robes (cf. Num. 15:38–39; Deut. 22:12). Just touching the tassels brought healing to the sick (Mark 5:28).

Living It Out

Jesus calls people to ministry so they can shepherd his people. If one is a pastor without a true love for people, they are not a pastor but only a lecturer. If one leads worship without a heart for people, they are a musician but not a worship pastor. If a person is a church staff member that watches the clock for quitting time, they are an employee but not a shepherd. If one is a church member without a love for fellow believers, they are an attender, not a part of the body.

Finally, like the disciples, we have a tendency to limit what God will do by assuming what is and is not possible for him. We look at our resources, whatever they may be, and say, "It can't be done." We must learn that God will not work if we give nothing, but when we give him everything, even though it is not enough, he can use our effort in a greater way than we could ever imagine.

Graceless Religion

Mark 7:1–23

The Big Picture

After the eye-opening demonstrations of Jesus' miraculous power in chapters 5–6, Mark provides a pause in the action by telling another story of confrontation between Jesus and the Pharisees and scribes. Jesus' ministry was met by determined resistance led by the Pharisees and scribes. Unable to overcome Jesus directly, they turn their gaze to his disciples. After setting the scene (Mark 7:1–4), Mark introduces Jesus' opponents' question (7:5) followed by his lengthy response (7:6–23). The first part of his response centers on two Old Testament passages and a twofold attack on the Pharisees' traditions (7:6–8, 9–13). In the second part of this section, Jesus teaches about what does and does not truly defile a person (7:14–23).

Digging In

The setting indicates the Pharisees and the scribes came from Jerusalem as an official delegation to investigate Jesus (7:1–2). The fact that they are gathered around him sounds ominous. Mark provides a parenthetical explanation in verses 3 and 4 to explain the debate over the washing of hands since his non-Jewish readers would not have understood what the problem was. The "traditions of the elders" were believed by the Pharisees to have been given to Moses on Mount Sinai along with the written law. They were written down around AD 200 in the Mishna, one of the key sources for understanding ancient Jewish practices.

The issue is not that Jesus' disciples were eating and their hands were dirty, but that the disciples failed to wash them in a ritual manner, cleansing themselves from ceremonial defilements. They had likely come into contact in the marketplace with people who had little concern for ritual purity, and thus, they were in some sense "contaminated." In the Old Testament, priests were to wash their hands in a prescribed way before they ate the holy bread, but the Pharisees extended this to all God's people.

You should notice the references to the "tradition of the elders" and related phrases in the passage (vv. 3, 5, 7, 8, 9, 13). Mark indicates that their question to Jesus is not sincere but deceitful. They point to Jesus' disciples as if he were responsible for everything they did and did not do. However, make no mistake, Jesus was the one they were interested in condemning.

Jesus exposes their hypocrisy in verses 6–13. He begins by quoting Isaiah 29:13, which deals with the absurdity of equating manmade rules with God's commands. He draws out his logical conclusion in verse 8, which reveals how they value their manmade rules over God's Word.

Jesus illustrates his thought by pointing to the Corban vow (7:9–13). God's Word indicates that one is to honor their parents and not speak ill of them (Exod. 20:12; 21:17; Deut. 5:16). In contrast to the clear teaching of God, the Pharisees taught, "If anyone tells his father or mother: Whatever benefit you might have received from me is corban." In a parenthetical comment, Mark explains the word for his Gentile readers as meaning "that is, an offering devoted to God." The vow allowed people to avoid the obligation to assist their parents by dedicating some of their resources to God, thus disregarding and dishonoring their needy parents. The result was a clear act of disobedience to God's commandment.

In verses 14–16, Jesus turns his attention to the crowds and provides a second argument against the Pharisees. He warns them that they must be careful to guard their hearts lest they become like the Pharisees. The reference to the heart is a metaphor for the seat of moral decision-making. How a person eats (with clean or unclean hands) and what a person eats (clean or unclean food) affects only the digestive tract, so what they eat has no bearing on the moral issues of the soul.

Jesus turns his attention to his disciples in verses 17–23. The issue at hand is the heart—"guard your heart." The disciples question Jesus about his previous comments. Jesus rebukes them for their failure to understand his clear and straightforward point concerning the heart. The issue is not what goes into a person's stomach but what comes out of their heart. Mark includes the parenthetical thought that Jesus declared all foods clean in verse 19. In verses 20–23, Jesus teaches that what comes out of a person (indwelling sin) is what defiles them. The sins Jesus lists remind us of how desperately we need a new heart that comes through the new birth.

Living It Out

I want us to consider two important points from today's study. Let's begin by focusing on the concluding verses of the passage. First, the heart, the very center of a person's being, must be carefully guarded. In the Sermon on the Mount, Jesus teaches "the pure in heart will see God." The greatest commandment is "Love the Lord your God with all your heart, soul, mind, and strength" (your entire being). An important question for all of us is, "What's the condition of our heart?" Is our heart soft, pliable, and sensitive to the Spirit of God?

A second matter has to do with the danger of becoming like the Pharisees. The Pharisees were men who knew the Scriptures and were zealous for pious practices like tithing, fasting, and prayer. They were faithful to worship in the synagogue on the Sabbath. Yet they were the major opposition to the ministry of Jesus and instrumental in his crucifixion. We should beware whenever we emphasize outward conformity to rules without a heartfelt passion for God; we are in danger of walking in the footsteps of the Pharisees. Whenever we find ourselves looking down on others as being less spiritual because they don't appreciate our religious preferences, when our preferences are part of traditionalism without a biblical mandate, we are in danger of Pharisaism. God's grace is the only antidote and protection against Pharisaism.

Jesus Does All Things Well!

Mark 7:24–37

The Big Picture

The discussion of clean and unclean food from the previous day's reading prepares us for the two stories we will examine today. In these two passages, Jesus demonstrates that there is no such thing as clean and unclean people when it comes to his ministry. In the previous passage, he declared all foods clean (Mark 7:19), and now, he declares all people clean. Jesus' ministry takes him to people who live on life's fringes.

Digging In

This is the third major exorcism story in Mark's Gospel (7:24–30; cf. 1:21–28; 5:1–20) and the second exorcism of a demon from a Gentile. As to how the girl became demonized, we simply do not know. One possibility, however, is the connection to the false religion of Tyrian people. The setting is the coastal city of Tyre, located in modern-day

Lebanon. People came from Tyre earlier in Jesus' ministry to see him perform miracles. This explains how he would have been known to them (cf. 3:7–8). Tyre is a two-day journey northwest from Galilee into Syria. Tyre was a traditional enemy of Israel.

Jesus wished to remain anonymous, but by this time in his ministry, that is hardly possible. He is confronted by a desperate mother from the region whose daughter had a demon. She doesn't describe how she knows her daughter is demonized. Her predicament is heart-wrenching. Mark tells us that she "fell at his feet." A couple of things are going on here. First, Mark describes Jesus taking the disciples outside their comfort zone. He is teaching them that in the future they are to take the gospel to all people. Second, this woman was thoroughly convinced that Jesus could cast the demon out of her daughter. She engages Jesus in a lively exchange. Jesus' words seem rather harsh and condescending. Jewish people often referred to Gentiles as "dogs." Jesus was testing her faith. How easily could she be put off or discouraged from pursuing Jesus on behalf of her daughter?

The woman would not be put off so easily. She believed Jesus could heal her daughter by casting out the demon, and she did not intend to leave until he did so. The woman's response was insightful: "Lord, even the dogs under the table eat the children's crumbs." Her point is that even the Gentiles were to benefit from the Messiah's coming. Jesus casts out the demon without being in the presence of the girl and apparently without even a word. No wonder the demons cowered in fear in his presence! When the mother returns home, she finds her daughter resting peacefully in her bed and "the demon was gone."

The next story takes place in Gentile territory as well (7:31–37). From Tyre, Jesus made his way to the Decapolis. The route he took was a little bit circuitous. Sidon was twenty-five miles north of Tyre, so Jesus first travels north and then to the eastern side of the Sea of Galilee and finally to the Decapolis ("ten cities"). Once again, the region is predominantly a Gentile region. Jesus continues to prepare his disciples for ministry outside their comfort zone.

A man who was deaf and as a result had trouble speaking was brought to Jesus for healing. Mark carefully describes Jesus' actions culminating in the man's healing. Rather than perform the healing publicly, Jesus takes the man away to handle the matter privately. Jesus' actions seem bizarre to us. We must be reminded, however, that Jesus could have healed him without speaking a word. He may have healed the man in this way to help stimulate the man's faith. He didn't always heal the same way. On other occasions, Jesus merely spoke, and people were healed.

What's more important is that Jesus looked toward heaven, sighed deeply, and said, "*Ephphatha!*" Mark adds a translation of the Aramaic word for his Gentile readers, "Be opened!" The healing was immediate with both the man's speech and hearing cured.

Jesus' ministry fulfilled Messianic expectations as seen in Isaiah 35:5–6:

> Then the eyes of the blind will be opened,
> and the ears of the deaf unstopped.
> Then the lame will leap like a deer,
> and the tongue of the mute will sing for joy,
> for water will gush in the wilderness,
> and streams in the desert.

The crowd responds in amazement declaring, "He has done everything well!"

Taking a moment to compare and contrast the two stories may be helpful. In the first story, the main character is a woman with a demonized daughter and the second is a deaf man with a speech impediment. In both stories, those who benefited from our Lord's ministry were people on the outside of traditional Judaism. In the first story, the woman was of the Syrophoenician race and in the second story, a Gentile from the Decapolis. Jesus is going places and helping outsiders to teach his disciples that the gospel is for all people. In both stories, Jesus does the seemingly impossible. In the first, he casts a demon out of a girl from a distance, and in the second, he heals a man who is deaf and has a speech impediment.

Living It Out

Jesus wants to press us out of our comfort zone. He went to hard places and ministered to people on the fringes of Jewish society and even outside Judaism. He may not call us to go to Tyre, but he certainly wants us to look around our neighborhood, work place, and family gatherings to share his name. Another implication is that we should never be surprised by what Jesus does in response to our heartfelt prayers. In the first story, Jesus responded to the intercession of a mother, and in the second story to a group of friends. Maybe you are discouraged and feel hopeless today over the condition of a loved one or friend. Maybe the circumstances of life are crushing the joy out of your soul. Draw hope, courage, strength, and resolve from the example of this woman.

The final words of the passage are particularly powerful—"he has done everything well." They spoke far better than they could have ever imagined. Of course, Jesus does all things well! Presently we see in a mirror dimly. The events of our lives seem confusing and not a little disappointing. We don't understand the "why" and the "how." A day is coming when we will look back over the course of our lives and see how God's plan has been perfectly executed. But until that day, we must walk by faith.

Day Fifteen

Overcoming Spiritual Blindness

Mark 8:1–21

The Big Picture

How soon we forget! Most of us are slow learners about the things of God. But we are in good company because so were the disciples. Our reading today has three sections—the two outer sections examine the disciples' failure to understand (Mark 8:1–10; 14–21) and the center section emphasizes the religious leaders' refusal to believe (8:11–13).

Digging In

Mark makes reference once again to a large crowd. The last reference to a large crowd was at the feeding of the five thousand (6:34). Jesus showed compassion to the people then because they were like sheep without a shepherd. Here again, we find a large crowd being described as having "nothing to eat" and he is moved by compassion. The two feeding stories are quite similar but with obvious distinctions. All four Gospels report the feeding of the five thousand (6:35–44;

Matt. 14:13–21; Luke 9:10–17; John 6:1–15), but only Mark and Matthew (Matt. 15:32–39) record the feeding of the four thousand.

The disciples remind us how easy it is to forget God's past faithfulness to us in the midst of present challenges (8:1–10). The probable location of the feeding means the crowd would have likely included both Jewish and Gentile people. Mark continues the theme that Jesus came to be the Savior of all people. The previous two miracles were performed for Gentiles.

Jesus is moved by compassion toward the crowd because they had been with him for three days and they no longer have anything to eat. Without feeding them, he fears many of them may be too weak to travel to their home. The disciples assess the situation and come to the settled conclusion that they cannot possibly get enough bread to feed them in such a desolate location.

In verses 4–9, we see, once again, how Jesus can do the seemingly unimaginable. The disciples recognize the impossible nature of the situation but fail to remember what Jesus did earlier in a similar situation. A good memory is one key to less worry! The disciples' frustration reveals their spiritual dullness. They knew God provided manna in the wilderness for his people in Moses' day (Exod. 16). They were now in the presence of one far greater than Moses (cf. 9:5–7). However, they still did not understand (cf. 6:52). Even so, Jesus worked through them to bring physical food for the crowd. What they clearly could not do by themselves, the Son of God did through them.

After learning how many loaves they have, Jesus gives thanks to God, breaks the bread, and has the disciples distribute it. The language is reminiscent of Jesus' words at the Last Supper (cf. 14:22–25). Mark next describes Jesus blessing the few small fish available to them and the disciples serving the people.

The people ate until they were full (8:8–9). After the earlier feeding, there were twelve baskets of leftovers collected, and after the feeding of the four thousand, there were seven large baskets of leftovers collected. Rather than sending the disciples away in a boat without him, as he did after the previous feeding, he dismissed the crowds and got into a boat with the disciples traveling to the district of Dalmanutha.

The second scene in this section is another hostile encounter with the Pharisees (8:11–13).[6] The request for a sign was an obstinate testing of the Son of God. They sought for a sign that would go beyond a healing, an exorcism, a resuscitation, or even a nature miracle. They demand Jesus perform a sign that demonstrates beyond any reasonable doubt that he came from God. Their request in light of Jesus' earlier miracles is absurd.

Jesus was grieved by their request, "Sighing deeply in his spirit." Their "demand" for a sign indicated that their hearts were so hard that no miracle would ever satisfy them. Jesus would not be forced into proving himself to a people who simply would not believe in him. For those whose hearts were open, Jesus' miracles were clear and irrefutable evidence that he was the Messiah.

Mark returns to Jesus and the disciples (8:14–21). The passage is not unrelated to the previous story. In some ways, the disciples are like the Pharisees in the sense that they don't see as clearly as they should see. The difference is the disciples followed Jesus rather than trying to trap him.

The disciples completely misunderstand Jesus' warning about the leaven of the Pharisees and Herod. They thought he was bothered by the fact that they had brought only one loaf of bread with them in the boat. Jesus' twofold reference "Watch out!" and "Beware" reveals how serious he is about this danger. Jesus is pointing his disciples back to the Pharisees' request for a sign, demonstrating their unbelief and hardness of heart. The reference to Herod refers to the danger of longing for political power.

Leaven, or yeast, causes dough to rise. Only a little leaven is required once it is worked into the dough. Jesus' point is that his people must not nurture their "little sins" because they will become "big ones." Paul wrote, "Don't you know that a little leaven leavens the whole batch of dough?" (1 Cor. 5:6). Jesus asks eight questions in rapid-fire succession that rebuke the disciples (8:17–21). The disciples, of all people, should know that a scarcity of bread is not a problem for Jesus. Although they saw the feeding miracles, they still do not grasp their implications. Jesus quotes Jeremiah 5:21 in reference to the disciples' inability to see. The final question, "Don't you understand yet?" suggests that a time is coming when they will understand. Mark's readers knew the disciples would understand at the time of Jesus' resurrection.

Living It Out

I want to direct our attention to two final thoughts as we consider how to live out the truths in the passage. First, remember God's past faithfulness to you as an encouragement to present faith in a difficult and seemingly impossible circumstance. Nothing is impossible with God! Second, don't make excuses for "little sins" because they never stay little. Like leaven, they will spread. A little leaven leavens the whole lump!

Life's Most Important Question

Mark 8:22–38

The Big Picture

The identity of Jesus is as controversial now as it was in his day. Mark was absolutely clear in his opening line that he believed Jesus to be the Christ and Son of God (Mark 1:1). Today's reading focuses on two key passages that are intended to help readers understand that while the disciples are growing in their understanding of who Jesus is, they still don't grasp his full identity. Yesterday's reading ended with Jesus asking the question, "Don't you understand yet?" (8:21). The answer in these passages is yes, but not fully.

Digging In

The first story is known as "the twice-touched blind man" (8:22–26). Only Mark records this miracle. The incident took place at Bethsaida on the east bank of the northeast shore of the Sea of Galilee where the Jordan River flows into it. The blind man is brought to Jesus and Jesus is begged "to touch him." Jesus leads him out of the village, spits on his eyes, and places his hands on him. After asking the man if he sees anything, the man responds that he sees people, but they look like trees walking. The second laying on of Jesus' hands results in the man seeing clearly. Mark gives no hint as to the reason for the gradual healing.

How are we to understand the fact that the man was not healed the first time Jesus touched him? In light of the previous passage (8:14–21), and the following one (8:27–30), this event seemingly is to be understood as an enacted parable, a real historical event intended to make a point much like a parable. The previous story described the disciples' failure "to see" or "understand." In the next scene, Peter confesses Jesus to be the Messiah but then rebukes him after Jesus predicts his suffering and death. The point being made is that the disciples are much like this twice touched blind man and need a "second touch." They will receive the second touch after Jesus' resurrection from the dead. The importance of the story is that the disciples' eyes are gradually opened.

This healing of the blind man continues to demonstrate the arrival of God's kingdom, pointing toward the coming restoration of all things. Several passages in Isaiah highlight this reality,

> Then the eyes of the blind will be opened and the ears of the deaf will be unstopped. Then the lame will leap like a deer, and the tongue of the mute will sing for joy, for waters will gush in the wilderness, and streams in the desert. (Isa. 35:5–6)

> On that day the deaf will hear words of a document, and out of a deep darkness the eyes of the blind will see. (Isa. 29:18)

> Then the eyes of those who see will not be closed, and the ears of those who hear will listen. (Isa. 32:3)

> In order to open blind eyes, to bring out prisoners from the dungeon and those sitting in darkness from the prison house. (Isa. 42:7)

The second event in this section records a monumental moment in Jesus' ministry and takes place at Caesarea Philippi (8:27–30). Here, one of Jesus' disciples confesses him for the first time in Mark's gospel to be the Messiah. Jesus keeps the disciples outside the hostile territory of Galilee and primarily in Gentile territory. The backdrop is Caesarea Philippi, a city renowned for its paganism and religious diversity. The city was built by Herod Philippi, son of Herod the Great, and was located at the base of Mount Hermon, twenty-five miles north of the Sea of Galilee. He named it in honor of Caesar and himself. The inhabitants were largely Gentile. The chief deity was the Roman god Pan. With this backdrop, Jesus asked, "Who do people say that I am?"

The multitudes have suggested that Jesus may be John the Baptist, Elijah, or one of the prophets. Each of these answers is laudatory, but a far cry from the Messiah and Son of God. Jesus then asks the disciples who they think him to be. Peter, speaking for the Twelve, declares boldly and confidently that Jesus is the Messiah. Strangely enough, Jesus tells them sternly that they are not to tell anyone. The probable reason is that Jesus does not want a premature confrontation with the Jewish leadership or the Roman government.

Jesus must now teach them what kind of Messiah he is. He refers to himself as "Son of Man" (8:31–33; cf. Dan. 7:13–14) and that he would suffer, be rejected, killed, and rise after three days. After taking Jesus aside, Peter rebukes him. Jesus' message certainly did not square with their messianic aspiration. The death of a messianic claimant was evidence that the person was not the messiah. They expected a conquering militaristic ruler. Like the twice-touched blind man, they don't see everything as clearly as they thought.

Jesus rebukes Peter sternly with the other disciples listening. Peter's attempt to keep Jesus from the cross was the same sort of temptation Jesus faced when Satan tried to keep Jesus from following God's will.

Jesus turns his attention to the crowd as well as his disciples. Those who desire to be his disciples must deny themselves, take up their cross, and follow him. His dramatic demands for those who wish to follow him are as stunning as the prediction of his death. He makes the stakes very clear in the next three verses. Heaven and hell are ultimately at stake. One can gain all the world has to offer but in doing so, loses everything. If a person chooses the world, then they demonstrate they are ashamed of being a follower of Christ. Those who are ashamed of following Christ will one day be judged by him.

Living It Out

There are three thoughts I want us to consider in light of our reading today. First, God's plan was so shocking to the disciples that they could not grasp it. Paul called God's plan a mystery, that is, something mankind could not ever conceive unless revealed by God. God's Son, suffering, dying, and being raised on the third day was the means by which Christ crushed the serpent's head (Gen. 3:15). Truly, God's ways are not our ways!

Second, Jesus' question is as important today as it was in his day. Who a person believes Jesus to be determines their eternity. Those who believe Jesus to be the Son of God and follow him in discipleship will one day be welcomed into their eternal dwelling. Those who choose the worldliness of the world will one day be judged by him.

Third, discipleship is not optional for the Christian life. A genuine believer in Christ is a disciple. Discipleship is a divine gift. To deny ourselves, take up our cross, and follow Jesus is a blessing. Denial involves saying no to the self-principles of life, such as self-promotion and self-righteousness. Denial involves crucifying "the flesh with its passions and desires" (Gal. 5:24) and following Jesus wherever he leads us.

Mountaintop Glory and Real-World Ministry

Mark 9:1–29

The Big Picture

The transfiguration is "a preview of coming attractions," following immediately after Jesus' prediction of his death and call to discipleship (Mark 8:3–38). The timing likely is intended to be a word of encouragement to his followers. However, in the two scenes immediately following the transfiguration, the discussion concerning the death of John the Baptist and the boy possessed by a demon, the disciples are reminded that the kingdom has not yet fully arrived.

Digging In

The chapter begins with a perplexing comment. This verse has been interpreted in a number of ways. Some understand the statement to be a reference to Jesus' resurrection and others to the Day of

Pentecost. However, the context likely points forward to the transfiguration event. Mark connects the transfiguration to the previous events with the statement "after six days." Mark doesn't want us to miss this connection between the call to discipleship and suffering with the glory depicted here.

Jesus is accompanied by Peter, James, and John. The likely location is Mount Hermon about 12–14 miles from Caesarea Philippi. The mountain rises to about 9,400 feet above sea level. Luke tells us that Jesus went there to pray (Luke 9:28). With typical Markan simplicity, he states, "he was transfigured in front of them." We get our word *metamorphosis* from the word translated "transfigured." The verb only occurs four times in the New Testament (Matt. 17:2; Rom. 12:2; 2 Cor. 3:18). In each instance, a radical change or transformation is displayed. Verse 3 describes the change that took place, noting "his clothes became dazzling—extremely white as no launderer on earth could whiten them." For a brief moment, Jesus' true identity is allowed to shine forth in all his glory.

The appearance of Elijah and Moses is unexpected. Why these two Old Testament figures? Moses was the supreme lawgiver, and Elijah was the first of the great prophets. Their presence indicates that Jesus' death and resurrection fulfill the teaching in the Law and the Prophets. Moses was a prototype of Christ—the Messiah was to be a prophet like Moses (Deut. 18:18). Elijah was to be the forerunner of the Messiah (Mal. 4:4–6). Interestingly, both men were associated with mountains as well: Moses with Mount Sinai (Exod. 19) and Elijah with Mount Horeb (1 Kings 19). Both men also underwent dramatic transformations: Moses when his face shown with reflected glory (Exod. 34:29–35) and Elijah when he was taken up to heaven in a chariot of fire (2 Kings 2:11).

Peter is uncertain about what to say and instead of remaining silent makes an inappropriate statement placing Jesus on the same level as the two Old Testament figures. The bigger issue is that Peter is looking at the circumstance from a human perspective rather than a divine perspective. Mark clarifies that Peter's words were the result of fear.

God's perspective is heard in verse 7, "This is my beloved Son, listen to him." Listen to him about what? What he has just said to them about his death and resurrection. Suddenly Jesus is alone, and Moses and Elijah are gone. Toward the end of Peter's life, he wrote of this event in 2 Peter 1:16–18:

> For we did not follow cleverly contrived myths when we made known to you the power and coming of our Lord Jesus Christ; instead, we were eyewitnesses of his majesty. For he received honor and glory from God the Father when the voice came to him from the Majestic Glory, saying "This is my beloved Son, with whom I am well-pleased!" We ourselves heard this voice when it came from heaven while we were with him on the holy mountain.

The transfiguration was a momentary manifestation of the glory of Christ to be revealed at his Second Coming, encouraging his followers that glory comes after the cross!

As Jesus and the three disciples come down from this mountaintop experience, they return to real-world ministry (9:9–13). Jesus commands them to silence and hints at his coming death and resurrection. The thought of a dying and rising Messiah remains foreign to their thinking. The disciples ask about Elijah in light of his recent appearance. Elijah's coming was to precede the appearance of the Messiah (cf. Mal. 4:5–6). Jesus' reply indicates that John the Baptist fulfilled the role ascribed to Elijah. His point is that both his and John's deaths did not catch God off guard but were prophesied in the Old Testament.

Jesus returns to find his disciples embroiled in an argument with the Pharisees (9:14–29). When the crowd sees Jesus, they are amazed. The question is, why? Maybe it was his impeccable timing. In the very midst of the heated debate, Jesus arrives. More likely, they were amazed at his appearance as he comes down from the Mount of Transfiguration, reminiscent of Moses when he came down from Mount Sinai (Exod. 34:29–35).

The boy's father explains his son's condition to Jesus and the disciples' inability to drive the demon out. Jesus responds with great frustration. The question is with whom is he frustrated? I would surmise that his frustration is likely with the disciples. He has given them authority to cast out demons, and they have done so before, but now, they fail to cast the demon out of the boy.

Jesus' attention is now directed toward the father and his son. The moment the demon comes directly into Jesus' presence, it throws the boy into a violent convulsion. We need to understand that the convulsion is not epilepsy or some other sort of physiological condition but is the result of demonic activity.

Jesus questions the father about how long his son has been in this condition. You can hear the desperation in the father's voice. All he has ever known was a son who could not hear or speak. This family has never known the joy that families experience through singing and playing with their children. Their world was shrouded in deep, dark hopelessness until they heard about Jesus.

The depth of the father's hopelessness is heard in his words, "have compassion on us." All he knows to ask for and all he wants now is pity. Jesus' words inspire a spark of hope in the father's hopeless heart. "Everything is possible . . ." (v. 23). Raw honesty fills the father's words when he responds, "I do believe, help my unbelief!"

As a crowd begins to gather, Jesus casts the demon out of the boy. Jesus refuses to give the devil a future opportunity to enter the boy again. The expulsion was somewhat violent. When Jesus is alone with the disciples, he explains why they were not able to cast the demon out. Jesus tells them that this kind of demon cannot come out by anything except by prayer. Jesus' words are a reminder of the power of intercessory prayer in doing battle with the enemy.

Living It Out

Paul uses the word *transformed* in 2 Corinthians 3:18, "We all, with unveiled faces, are looking as in a mirror at the glory of the Lord and are being transformed into the same image from glory to glory; this is from the Lord who is the Spirit." The transfiguration of Jesus foreshadowed the glory in which he will appear at his Second Coming and is a reminder to us that who we are now is not who we will become! When life and ministry are hard and disappointing, we need to remember that this is not the end.

Service, not Self-Seeking

Mark 9:30–50

The Big Picture

In this section, Jesus continues to focus on discipleship as he moves toward Jerusalem. This series of interactions show the disciples' continued inability to understand and their self-centeredness. The main thought is that discipleship demands becoming like Jesus in self-sacrificial service to others. His followers must reject exclusivity and resist sin and temptation in their lives.

Digging In

Jesus returns to Galilee from the territory of Herod Philip. Notice that he is focusing on his disciples (Mark 9:31–32). This second passion prediction adds the issue of betrayal. Still, they fail to understand and were afraid to ask any questions about his betrayal or death. Significantly, the following discussion happened on the heels of Jesus' passion prediction (9:33–37). In this passion prediction, as well as in the previous one, Jesus connects his death and discipleship. Discipleship is not optional. If one receives the saving benefits of his death, they must follow in discipleship.

The disciples' discussion on greatness illustrates how completely mistaken they were in their thinking. The discussion takes place back in Capernaum. Jesus, aware of their earlier discussion, asks what they had been discussing. Aware of the inappropriateness of the discussion, they remain silent. Jesus sits down, taking the position of a teacher. He directs his comments to the disciples on the subject of greatness. He turns the world's approach to greatness on its head. Those who wish to be first must be last and the servant of all. To illustrate his point, he takes a child to demonstrate what is meant to be servant of all. A child was incapable of furthering anyone's ministry or cause. In this sense, they are "least of all." So, to welcome a child in humble service is to welcome Jesus, and to welcome Jesus is to welcome the Father. The implications of servanthood are great!

The subject of discipleship continues in the following verses (9:38–50). Perhaps the awkwardness of the situation causes John to speak out of turn. He demonstrates the very exclusivity Jesus has just condemned. How strange that they rebuff someone casting out a demon in Jesus' name when they themselves had just failed to do it (cf. 9:14–29). These are John's only recorded words in Mark's gospel.

Jesus' response indicates that whoever performs a miracle "in his name"—that is, by Christ's power and for his glory, is not against them but is with them. The same is true for those who give a cup of cold water in Christ's name—for his glory—they too will receive a reward, which is the only reference to reward in Mark's gospel. What a glorious thought! Jesus does not overlook or minimize a cup of cold water given in his name. Blessed be the name of the Lord!

The theme of discipleship continues as Jesus discusses the pursuit of holiness and the danger of habitual sin (9:42–48). Jesus uses hyperbole to emphasize the danger of sin and the radical approach that must be taken to overcome it. We must hate our sin so much that we will act decisively against it.

In verse 42, the danger is external, that is, someone leading a younger believer into sin. However, in the following verses the temptations arise from within. We should notice there are only two alternatives—entering the kingdom or Gehenna.[7] Jesus speaks of hell as a real place. We should not think that Jesus is suggesting that a true believer can lose their salvation or that he is teaching sinless perfection. We will never be sinless on this side of heaven. However, for a professing believer to be unconcerned about habitual sin is to call into question the reality of their salvation.

The final verses deal with the pursuit of holiness and the reality of suffering (9:49–50). Every disciple in this life will undergo the fire of suffering, disappointment, and persecution. Believers are not exempt from living in a fallen world. In fact, God uses fire to purify our faith. He doesn't waste our heartache and disappointments. According to Jesus, salt is good. Salt refers to the purity of a disciple, and once the disciple compromises their faith, their usefulness is damaged.

Living It Out

As we conclude our reading for today, there are a couple of thoughts about serving others and pursuing holiness we need to consider. First, we see that the desire for prominence resides in even the best of hearts. The disciples that have left everything to follow Jesus have yet to grasp the heart of Jesus on the issues of servanthood, which does not come to us naturally. We must fight the yearnings for prominence and pride of place and seek to serve others. Secondly, those who love Jesus will seek, by his grace and for his glory, to be people committed to holy living. They will seek to put to death the deeds of the flesh and to live as Christ's disciples.

Marriage, Children, and Possessions

Mark 10:1–31

The Big Picture

The episodes in Mark 10 unfold in a mostly chronological sequence as Jesus draws ever closer to Jerusalem. Thematically, the concept of discipleship continues as Jesus touches on marriage and divorce, children (Mark 10:1–16), and the danger of riches (10:17–31).

Digging In

As Jesus marches toward Jerusalem, the crowds continue to gather and listen to his teaching. Once again, some Pharisees try to trap him by asking him a difficult question on the subject of divorce. Among the Pharisees, there was a debate between two schools of thought on the issue. One view limited grounds for divorce to sexual unfaithfulness, and the other allowed divorce for any number of reasons.

Jesus turns their discussion to Scripture, asking them to consider what Moses taught. They respond by giving a summary of Deuteronomy

24:1. Jesus does not question the law, but his answer reaches back to God's first principles found in Genesis 2:24. Moses' permission of divorce was an accommodation to human sin, an attempt to bring some sort of order in a society that disregarded God's standards. That, however, was not God's original intention for marriage. His initial design for marriage was one man and one woman for a lifetime. The rabbis seem to have mistaken God's gracious provision in allowing divorce as his approval of it.[8]

Family issues continue with the discussion of the place of children in the kingdom community in the second passage on children (cf. 9:36–37). Parents bringing their children to a rabbi to receive a blessing was common. Mark does not tell us why the disciples rebuked the parents; although the perceived low status of children and the feeling that Jesus was too busy to be bothered is likely the reason. With one simple statement, "Let the little children come to me," Jesus highlights the importance of children to God.

Jesus goes on to use children to illustrate two kingdom truths. First, the phrase "such as these" means that the kingdom "belongs to" those who are considered insignificant (like children). Jesus has come for the lowly and rejected in this world. Second, the kingdom belongs to those who become like children; those who model vulnerability, trust, dependence, and openness to the gospel. Jesus then takes the children into his arms and blesses them.

In 10:17–31, Jesus moves from blessing children, who had very little status, to engaging a rich man. This man appears to ask a genuine question from a sincere heart. This individual is commonly known as the "rich young ruler," which is a composite description coming from the Synoptic Gospels. Matthew tells us that he was "young" (Matt. 19:20), and Luke tells us that he was a "ruler" (Luke 18:18). His wealth is mentioned in all three Synoptic Gospels. Jesus' response indicates that a person's priorities portray their heart.

The man's question on what he must do to inherit eternal life seems sincere enough. Jesus' initial response, however, is a bit surprising. He responds to the man's statement, "Good teacher," with a question of his own, "Why do you call me good?" Jesus is not denying his own goodness. He understands the man to believe that he himself is a "good man" addressing another good man. Jesus wants him to realize that no one should focus on their own "goodness" when considering eternal life. Salvation comes only from God, who alone is good. He must focus on God, not on himself.

Jesus directs the man's attention to the second table of the Ten Commandments. Jesus does not mention the prohibition to covetousness. The man believes that he has been fastidiously keeping the commandments from his youth. He is claiming to be a faithful follower of God. Jesus, however, forces the man to look more deeply into his own heart, thus revealing the hold his possessions have on him. Jesus calls the man to make a radical choice. Only when he gives up the claims the world holds on him will he find true life. When he breaks these ties with worldliness, he will become a follower of Jesus.

He goes away very sad because he is very wealthy and has chosen the priority of worldly wealth over eternal life. In private, Jesus explains to the disciples that the wealthy tend to trust in their wealth above all else, which can blind them to their need of a Savior. The disciples are astonished at Jesus' teaching. Speaking hyperbolically, Jesus says, "It's easier for a camel to go through the eye of a needle than for a rich person to be saved." The statement is somewhat humorous as one attempts to picture cramming a large camel through the tiny opening of a needle. Yet, what is impossible with men is possible with God, as seen in Luke's gospel with the conversion of Zaccheus (Luke 19:1–10).

Peter, speaking for the disciples, says they have done exactly what this wealthy ruler was unwilling to do and left everything to follow him. While following Jesus has been quite costly, Jesus promises they will be amply blessed in this present age and in the one to come. Those who have been rejected by family and friends will find a multitude of new family members and friends in the kingdom. They will experience the eternal life which the rich ruler rejected. What is unexpected is the reference to "persecutions." Jesus' disciples must understand that divine blessing does not mean an absence of trials, afflictions, and persecutions in this world. Verse 31 provides a fitting conclusion to the section ("many who are first will be last, and the last first").

Living It Out

As we consider the myriad of topics Jesus touches on in this passage, one that stands out is Jesus' deep love for sinners. We must never forget that Jesus feels love and compassion for the souls of unbelievers—whether they are children, the extremely rich, or those who are terribly poor.

There is no doubt that he has a special love for his followers, his bride. But Jesus has a very big heart. He is filled with pity, compassion, and tender concern even for those like the rich young ruler. We should never forget how he wept over the city of Jerusalem before the Triumphal Entry (Luke 19:41–44). However, despite his love for the ruler, he would not lower his call for repentant faith. Jesus does not require every would-be-follower to sell everything and physically leave everyone and everything to follow him. But he does call all to repent and believe in the gospel (Mark 1:15).

A Peculiar Kind of Greatness

Mark 10:32–52

The Big Picture

These are the final events in Jesus' public ministry before the beginning of Passion Week. Jesus' journey to Jerusalem in Mark's gospel has centered on two major topics: his passion predictions and discipleship. The passion prediction in today's reading is the final and most detailed of the three. Jesus' teaching on discipleship here continues to focus on servanthood and suffering. The disciples fail again to understand what Jesus means by servanthood and instead focus on seeking greatness. Bartimaeus focuses on Jesus and is healed and then follows Jesus in discipleship.

Digging In

The final verse of the previous passage serves as a bridge between the two sections, concluding yesterday's reading but, in another sense, introducing today's reading. Jesus' death set forth in the third passion prediction is the perfect example of what is meant by, "many who are first will be last, and the last first" (Mark 10:31). Jesus leads the way as he marches on to Jerusalem. Those following him are astonished and afraid because they know that the religious leaders in Jerusalem are out to get him. Jesus' courage is undeniable. He takes his disciples aside and tells them for the third time what will happen in Jerusalem (10:32–34).

Jesus is no sooner finished with his passion prediction when James and John approach him about positions of authority in the kingdom. Talk about misunderstanding what Jesus just said! They want seats of prominence—one on the right and the other on the left. Later, at Jesus' crucifixion, one person is crucified on his right and the other on his left (15:27). Mark may be suggesting that the latter is the true place of glory in the kingdom. Jesus predicts suffering and death for them instead of worldly glory. In fact, James will be the first apostle martyred (Acts 12:2) and John will one day be exiled to Patmos.

Jesus uses the opportunity to teach, once again, on servant-leadership (10:41–45). While they had been over this terrain before, this teaching is a very hard lesson to learn. We see that the desire for prominence resides in even the best of hearts. The disciples who left everything to follow Jesus have yet to grasp the heart of Jesus on the issues of leadership and service. They think about leadership from a worldly mind-set—like the Gentiles whose rulers lord over those under them. They see leadership from the perspective of being served, but Jesus sets forth a model where the leader is the one who serves.

Jesus' work on the cross is the perfect example of what is meant for the first to be the servant of all. Jesus' ransom statement uses a metaphor to describe our predicament and his sacrifice. The ransom image suggests that we are enslaved and cannot possibly ever pay for our own freedom. Someone else must pay. Jesus' death is not a tragic accident or a courageous act of martyrdom, but a sacrificial death for sinners. Clearly, we cannot save ourselves. Jesus paid our debt. In light of his sacrifice for us, how can we seek greatness for ourselves?

The following passage should not be seen as completely disconnected from what we have just read (10:46–52). We read in these verses an account of the last healing miracle in Mark. We discover that while the disciples see physically, they don't yet have clear spiritual sight. The very opposite is true with Bartimaeus. He is physically blind, but his spiritual sight is clear.

Jesus, his disciples, and a large crowd of pilgrims were leaving Jericho when they encounter blind Bartimaeus ("son of Timaeus") sitting by the roadside begging. We don't learn the names of many of the people Jesus encountered in this gospel, so he must have been a memorable person. His plight was a sad one. In the ancient world, his day would have been filled with horrible boredom—sitting, begging, and little else. If he were fortunate, he would be placed at a busy intersection.

Apparently, he had heard about Jesus. His one opportunity to beg him for healing had arrived. The unusual thing is that he recognized Jesus of Nazareth as the "Son of David." The only time in the gospel that this title is ascribed to Jesus is by a blind beggar. While he was blind physically, he had a deep appreciation of Jesus' true identity.

The crowd's indifference toward him turns to frustration, and they try to silence him. But he is a man of resilience and not easily put off. He cries out all the louder for mercy! While the crowd just passed him by, like they did every day, Jesus stops when he hears a solitary cry for mercy.

When Bartimaeus heard the words, "He's calling you," his heart must have leaped into his throat. In the midst of a celebratory and raucous crowd, Jesus hears the cry of a single voice. Jesus asks him the most important question he has ever been asked, "What do you want me to do for you?" This is the same question he asked James and John a few days earlier. His answer is brief and to the point, "I want to see." There was no doubt about what he was asking of Jesus.

Jesus senses that there is more inside this man than meets the eye. He has faith that has sprung to life in a once hopeless heart. "Your faith has saved you"—his sight is restored, and his heart is converted. Notice that he does what every disciple must do—he follows Jesus, the very thing that the rich young ruler refused to do.

Living It Out

I want us to consider two final thoughts from today's reading. First, the Lord places a peculiar standard of greatness before the disciples. His standard is the exact opposite of what the world teaches and strives after. Our Lord's teaching instructs us that his ways are the opposite of the world's ways. The world's desire is to receive honor and acclaim, but Jesus wants his disciples to focus on service to people.

A second insight is how easy it is to pass by seemingly expendable people. We see people in need and yet often do not notice them. Do you hear the cry of the hurting? Seldom do we know what God may be doing inside these people we no longer see. Let's pray that God would give us the eyes and ears of Jesus.

Day Twenty-One

The Triumphal Entry

Mark 11:1–11

The Big Picture

The pace of Mark's gospel slows down considerably when Jesus reaches Jerusalem. Approximately forty percent of his gospel focuses on the final week of Jesus' life. This week is often called "Holy Week" and is the culmination of Jesus' life's work. The reason he came was to die for sin and be raised on the third day. Mark is careful to delineate the chronology of the week in a way he has not done earlier in his gospel. The beauty of this treatment is that it allows us to follow Jesus' path from the Triumphal Entry to the empty tomb during Easter week each year.

Jesus' time in Jerusalem met anticipated opposition that grows to a fever pitch as the week progresses. The opening events of the week function as prophetic object lessons—the Triumphal Entry, the cleansing of the temple, and the cursing of the fig tree. These three prophetic actions foreshadow Israel's disastrous future culminating with the destruction of the city in AD 70.

Digging In

Jesus' journey to Jerusalem has ended. The culmination of his life's work is at hand. The Triumphal Entry occurred one week before resurrection Sunday. Believers have celebrated this day throughout Christian history as Palm Sunday. Jesus may have entered Jerusalem through what is now called St. Stephen's gate, near the north entrance of the outer court of the temple.

In verses 1–7, Mark describes the preparation made for his entry. Passover pilgrims commonly arrived a week beforehand to purify themselves and make the necessary preparations. Bethany is located on the road to Jericho about two miles east of Jerusalem. Jesus stays there during Passion Week (Mark 11:11–12; 14:3–9). Bethphage was a little-known village located in the vicinity of Jerusalem.

The Mount of Olives is situated to the east of the temple mount and overlooks it, offering a beautiful panoramic view of the city. The Mount of Olives is frequently associated with final judgment and the place where the Messiah would manifest himself. Zechariah 14:4 reads,

> On that day his feet will stand on the Mount of
> Olives, which faces Jerusalem on the east. The Mount
> of Olives will be split in half from east to west, form-
> ing a huge valley, so that half the mountain will move
> to the north and half to the south.

Jesus now declares himself openly to be the Messiah as he fulfills Old Testament prophecies.

In Mark 11:2–3, Jesus instructs two of his disciples to go to a nearby village and retrieve a colt. He gives detailed instructions to them—where to find the colt and what to say if they are questioned about taking it.

Whether this incident exhibits Jesus' planning or his supernatural knowledge is difficult to know. Either way, the emphasis is on Jesus' control of the situation. Prearranging this event with the owner of the colt would explain his detailed instructions to his disciples and would also heighten the fact that Jesus had been planning for this moment for some time, thereby emphasizing its symbolic significance. Yet, the event is very possibly an example of Jesus' supernatural knowledge and sovereign control over these events. The best understanding likely is to understand this as another example of Jesus' supernatural knowledge.[9]

The fact that the colt had never been ridden means it was never used for a secular purpose and therefore suitable for a religious purpose. Both Matthew and John's Gospels emphasize the fact that this event fulfilled Zechariah 9:9 (Matt. 21:5; John 12:15). The passage reads,

> "Rejoice greatly, Daughter Zion!
> Shout in triumph, Daughter Jerusalem!
> Look, your King is coming to you;
> he is righteous and victorious,
> humble and riding on a donkey,
> on a colt, the foal of a donkey."

Clearly, Jesus intended to demonstrate to those with spiritual eyes to see that he indeed is the long-awaited Messiah. In verse 7, Jesus' followers place their cloaks on the donkey as an improvised saddle. Pilgrims did not normally ride into Jerusalem, but Jesus is no ordinary pilgrim nor is this entry ordinary. Centuries earlier, Solomon rode into Jerusalem on David's donkey to claim his throne (1 Kings 1:32–48). Not to be left out of the moment, many in the crowd spread their cloaks on the ground, and others spread branches as a sort of "red carpet" treatment. At this point, Jesus remains extremely popular with the people.

Accompanying pilgrims begin to cry out "Hosanna!" The pilgrims' words are taken from Psalm 118:25–26, a part of the Hallel Psalms (Pss. 113–118). These Psalms were sung by pilgrims as they entered Jerusalem at festivals such as Passover. The word *Hosanna* translates the Hebrew "Lord, save us!" The word may be a prayer asking God to establish his kingdom, or by the first century, it may just be an exclamation of joy similar to, "Praise the Lord!"

The words, "Blessed is he who comes in the name of the Lord!" also come from Psalm 118. The crowd continues, "Blessed is the coming kingdom of our father David!" When Jesus enters Jerusalem, he goes straight to the temple. The fact that he merely looks around appears somewhat anticlimactic.

Living It Out

The Triumphal Entry initiates both the tragedy and the glory of Passion Week. Jesus unveils, for those with eyes to see, his messianic identity. The words of the pilgrims were truer than they could have ever realized. Their heartfelt praise should inspire us to heartfelt worship of Jesus. Our praise and worship of him should exhibit an even greater devotion because we know "the whole story." What they knew only partially, we know fully. We should sing in congregational and private worship—loudly, boldly, passionately, and confidently because of what we believe about Jesus and how we feel toward him. While our emotions may rise and fall due to life's circumstances, what we know about Jesus, based on God's Word, should inspire us to sing with the crowds, "Hosanna!"

When Jesus Gets Mad

Mark 11:12–26

The Big Picture

As mentioned in yesterday's reading, Jesus begins Passion Week with three symbolic actions. At the Triumphal Entry, he publicly acknowledges his messianic identity. The second and third symbolic actions are intertwined in an A/B/A pattern: Jesus curses the fig tree (A); cleanses the temple (B); and then the withered fig tree is discovered (A). In these symbolic acts, Jesus presents himself as the eschatological judge.

Traditionally, the action in the temple has been called the cleansing of the temple; however, we should understand this act along the lines of the judgment of the temple. Both the fig tree and the temple stories have to do with the absence of fruit and God's coming judgment. The cursing of the fig tree and the condemnation of the temple both happen on Monday (Mark 11:12–19). The discovery that the fig tree has withered happens on the following morning (11:20–26).

Digging In

Jesus' hunger provides an opportunity for the second symbolic act. Fig trees typically sprout leaves in March and about the same time also begin to develop a green fig. In the Old Testament, Israel was sometimes compared to a fig tree or vineyard. Inevitably, Israel was condemned for its failure to produce fruit.

That we should understand the cursing of the fig tree as a symbolic act, or even a prophetic act, is seen in Mark's comment, "it was not the season for figs" (11:12–14). Figs were not harvested until later in the spring. Jesus knew that figs would not be ripened and therefore deliberately acted as he did to illustrate the meaning of the temple cleansing. Mark notes specifically that the disciples were listening when Jesus "cursed" the tree.

Jesus would have entered Jerusalem through the eastern gate since he was coming from Bethany. Herod's temple was one of the most beautiful temples in the ancient world. Jesus' actions take place in the court of the Gentiles. He demonstrates a righteous indignation for the merchandising activities taking place there. The Jewish people were required to pay a half-shekel temple tax annually (Exod. 30:11–16). Pilgrims had to exchange their coins for Tyrian coins because of the purity of the silver of the coins, which opened the door for charging exorbitant rates for the exchange. Furthermore, to bring animals from great distances for required sacrifices was too difficult and opened the door for exorbitant price gouging. In addition, people were apparently using the temple courts as a shortcut through the city.

Jesus condemned the practices because the court of the Gentiles, which should have been a place of prayer for all people, had been turned into a place of merchandising and a thoroughfare. Jesus' reference, "for all nations," likely comes from Isaiah 56:7. In Isaiah, this passage was part of the prophet's emphasis on the procession of the nations to Zion, the promise that, in the messianic age, all peoples of the earth would come and worship in the temple. The commercialism that they had brought into the temple was demeaning its very purpose.

There is also a deliberate contrast between "house of prayer" and "den of thieves." The latter phrase comes from Jeremiah 7:11, where

Jeremiah condemns the apostate nation for robbery, murder, immorality, idolatry, and for turning God's house into "a den of thieves." The unscrupulous motives of the leaders had brought down judgment upon God's people.

The religious leaders begin looking for a way to kill Jesus, but they fear him because of his popularity with the crowds. When evening comes, Jesus leaves the city and returns to Bethany. The next morning, on their way to Jerusalem, the disciples discover that the fig tree had withered (11:20–25). Jesus uses it as an opportunity to teach the disciples on the topics of prayer, faith, and forgiveness. Jesus' point is that God does great things in response to the prayer. When God's people pray, however, they must not harbor bitterness and ill will in their heart toward others. Bitterness is detrimental to believing prayer. Faith is demonstrated in both praying to God and forgiving others.

Living It Out

When Jesus arrived in Jerusalem, he came to the temple looking for fruit, but the religious establishment seemed to be concerned only with financial gain. Many radio and television ministries have become little more than a marketplace for religion. They spend more time trying to sell "ministry" items and "helps" than they do teaching the Word of God. The same is true in many Christian organizations where the leaders tend to live more like Fortune 500 CEOs than godly servant-leaders. A similar attitude can be said of many that sit in the pews, who are more enamored with their retirement portfolios than living for God's honor. Materialism and consumerism are two of Satan's biggest traps for Western Christianity.

The concluding verses of the passage are a magnificent incentive to prayer and forgiveness. The two are entwined. The bigger point is that God will do great things, speaking hyperbolically, like the casting of mountains into the sea, in response to the prayers of his people. Let's not fail to see God work because we fail to pray big prayers of him. Big prayers are asking God to do what only he can do and then giving him the glory for doing what is humanly impossible.

The Patience and Judgment of God

Mark 11:27–12:12

The Big Picture

The better part of Tuesday during Passion Week is a series of five controversies that take place in the temple court. Today's passage focuses on the leaders' attempt to embarrass Jesus before the crowds. Jesus, in response, explains the meaning of the clearing of the temple from the previous day. With each succeeding controversy, the religious leaders are humiliated before the crowds. These five controversy stories parallel the five earlier controversy stories in Mark 2:1–3:6.

Digging In

The first question from the leading priests, scribes, and elders relates to the cleansing of the temple (Mark 11:27–33). This group likely represents the seventy-one members of the Sanhedrin, the Jewish ruling council. They want to know who gave him authority to clear the temple as he did.[10]

Jesus responds by asking them a question concerning the origin of John's baptism—was it from God or man? The implicit point is that both John's baptism and Jesus' authority originated from God. As they confer, they realize that he has backed them into a corner. The people believed John to be a prophet from God. If they said his baptism was from men, then the crowds would stone them, but if they said from God, then why did they refuse to be baptized by him? Since they do not answer Jesus' question, he refuses to answer their question directly.

Jesus immediately goes on to tell the parable of the vine-growers to demonstrate both the patience and judgment of God (12:1–12). The background to this parable is Isaiah 5:1–7: "The Song of the Vineyard." The imagery would have been familiar to Jesus' audience: someone plants a vineyard, builds a lookout tower, puts a fence around the vineyard, and digs a pit for a wine vat. Mark's readers, and Jesus' audience, would have understood the story as an allegory condemning the Jewish leadership.

The main points are evident: the tenants represent Israel's leaders; the owner represents God; the servants represent the Old Testament prophets; the beloved son represents Jesus, the Son of God; the murder of the son represents Jesus' crucifixion; and the giving of the vineyard to others represents the judgment coming upon Israel and the establishment of the church. The interpretation would have been even clearer to Mark's readers than to Jesus' original audience, but the religious leaders understood clearly enough, and they sought to arrest him.

The first harvest would have come approximately four years after the vineyard was planted. The owner's share of the crop would have been either a certain quantity of grapes and wine or a financial payment for the lease of the vineyard. Old Testament prophets often are referred to as servants (Amos 3:7; Zech. 1:6). The owner's servants were repeatedly mistreated and killed by the leaders (1 Kings 18:13; 19:10, 14; Jer. 26:20–23; Neh. 9:26).

Surely, the tenants considered the fact that, at some point, they would have to pay for what they had done. But maybe the point is that they thought they could get away with what they were doing since they had not yet suffered any consequences for their actions. The tenants' thinking is not logical, but that is the issue. Sin is never logical!

Most people think that since they have not suffered any consequences for their sins, they have gotten away with those sins. They take God's patience for granted.

Finally, he sends his "beloved Son." This phrase has been used of Jesus on two earlier occasions (1:11; 9:7) and reflects the redemptive heart of God that he would send his beloved Son to die. One wonders what the tenants must have been thinking if they thought the vineyard would be theirs if they killed the owner's son. Again, their thinking does not make sense. Rejection of God's messengers and rejection of God's Son makes no sense.

The parable concludes with two rhetorical questions (12:9–11). The first, "What then will the owner of the vineyard do?" The owner of the vineyard is none other than God himself. Those who thought they controlled the vineyard find themselves cast out and the vineyard given to others. The second rhetorical question introduces Jesus' quote of Psalm 118:22–23. The rejected stone is the rejected Son. Interestingly enough, Psalm 118 is a thanksgiving hymn celebrating David's victory over his enemies and was quoted at the Triumphal Entry. David was a cornerstone—rejected but ultimately victorious. Jesus is *the* greater David—rejected by his countrymen but the cornerstone (cf. Acts 4:11; 1 Pet. 2:4, 6–7).

The religious leaders hated him and wanted to kill him because they knew that he spoke the parable against them. They failed to act because they were cowards. They would wait until the crowds weren't around and could act under the cover of darkness in the middle of the night in an olive grove just outside the city.

Living It Out

Not only do we see how illogical sin is, but we also see how patient God is. He sent prophets to his people over and over again, but they refused to listen. Finally, he sent his Son and they nailed him to a cross. God repeatedly called the nation back to himself, but most of them refused to listen. Has Jesus repeatedly reached out to you, and you still find yourself rejecting his gracious overtures? Perhaps he has reached out to you through words of admonition from parents, small group leaders, or the conviction of the Holy Spirit. Just as God's patience once ended in the parable of the vine growers and then came the judgment, so the same will be true with those who refuse to respond to God's gracious invitation.

Most of you reading this book obviously know Jesus. But, have you ever thought about how great an effort the Lord undertook so you could hear the message over and over again? This thought should challenge us in three ways. First, we should be willing to be a voice that delivers that message to others over and over again. Second, and along the same line, we should be as patient with others as the Lord was patient with us. Third, we should give praise and glory to God that he didn't quit—but sent his beloved Son for us!

Jesus on Government and Marriage

Mark 12:13–27

The Big Picture

The religious leaders continue to try and trap Jesus. In the two passages we study today, the first has to do with submission to government and the second with the doctrine of the resurrection from the dead. The vast differences of the two topics reveal Jesus' wisdom to deal with such a wide range of matters.

Digging In

Having failed in challenging Jesus' authority, his opponents try to alienate him from the crowd. The flattering of the Pharisees and Herodians is insincere, and they want to trap him into saying something that could lead to his arrest. Since they were not allies and disagreed on most issues, the presence of the Herodians with the Pharisees is odd. Earlier in 3:6, however, they agreed on the fact that Jesus needed to be killed.

They begin by flattering Jesus. The four insincere compliments describe Jesus' integrity, fairness, impartiality, and truthfulness. The irony is that what they did not truly believe about Jesus was actually true of him. Obviously, they are hoping to catch him off guard by their insincere comments. They question him about the paying of the poll tax. This particular tax was to be paid by all adults living in Judea under Roman rule. Interestingly enough, as a Galilean, Jesus was not responsible for paying the poll tax. The amount of the tax was one denarius annually. A denarius was equal to one day's wage for a common laborer. This tax was a very volatile issue in Judea.

Jesus is fully aware of their duplicity. They believe they have Jesus between a rock and a hard place. If he answers yes, then the crowds will be upset with him, and if he answers no, then he puts himself in opposition to the Roman government. Jesus responds by requesting that he be given a denarius, the very amount of the tax. The coin had the Emperor Tiberius' image on it. He reigned from AD 14–37. The coin also included the inscriptions, "Tiberius Caesar Augustus, son of [the] divine Augustus" on the one side and "high priest" on the other. The image on the coin was idolatrous and the inscriptions blasphemous. It is quite interesting that the religious leaders have one of the coins but Jesus does not.

Jesus' response is brilliant! "Give to Caesar the things that are Caesar's, and to God the things that are God's." His words cannot be taken as those of an anti-Roman zealot in opposition to Jewish taxation by Caesar. However, Jesus' statement cannot be understood as pro-Roman either, because service to God is fundamental, and God is ultimately over Caesar.[11]

Jesus goes from answering a question about taxes to the issue of the resurrection from the dead (Mark 12:18–27). The Sadducees were a priestly group whose base of power was the temple. They dominated the Sanhedrin, the Jewish high court, and were the group from which the High Priest was chosen. This passage is the only specific reference to them in Mark's gospel. The Sadducees did not believe in a future bodily resurrection from the dead.

The scenario they present to Jesus is a ridiculous application of the Old Testament law of levirate marriage. According to Old Testament law, when a man died without an heir, his brother had to marry the widow and produce children to carry on the family line. The first son of this marriage was considered the son of the dead brother (Deut. 25:5–6). Their purpose is to show the supposedly ridiculous concept of a future bodily resurrection from the dead (cf. Acts 4:1–2; 23:8).

Jesus points out two errors in their thinking (12:24–27). First, he rebukes the Sadducees because of their ignorance of the Scriptures. The resurrection of the dead is referred to most clearly in the Old Testament Prophets and Writings.[12] However, the Sadducees accepted only the Torah as ultimately authoritative (Genesis–Deuteronomy). Accordingly, Jesus answers them from the Torah. Jesus points to Moses's encounter with God at the burning bush (Exod. 3:6) and demonstrates that God's covenant with the patriarchs did not end at death. They were still alive, for God is the God of the living, and not the dead. God's covenant relationship with his people extends beyond their physical death, which means that the afterlife must be a reality.

Second, Jesus challenged the Sadducees' failure to understand God's power. The Sadducees assumed that the age to come would be an extension of the present age which is not true. God can give us bodies suitable for the present age, but he can also give us bodies suitable for an eternal age (1 Cor. 15:20–58). In this new existence, there is no need for sexual reproduction because there is no more death. Intimacy and marriage are superseded by fellowship of a multitude of fellow believers with one another and especially with God. In this sense, believers will be like the angels. Mark's readers knew that Jesus had conquered death.

Living It Out

There are still Sadducees in churches today. They know the Bible, but they have never experienced its transforming power. They know the teachings and the stories of the Bible, but they don't know the God of the Bible. We must read the Bible prayerfully, slowly, and reflectively—seeking the Scripture's meaning and its implications for our lives. We must then believe and obey the Bible's teachings. The Bible clearly teaches us that there is a coming resurrection from the dead for both the righteous and the unrighteous (cf. John 5:28–29). The hope of heaven is an incentive to keep our eyes on the things above, where Christ is seated (Col. 3:1–4). The Bible describes heaven using images such as a wedding; a dinner party; magnificent city; a beautiful garden; and a marvelous concert where all God's people are singing out in praise to God.

Loving God and Neighbor

Mark 12:28–34

The Big Picture

We continue our study of the questions put to Jesus on Tuesday of Holy Week. Today, we will examine a much smaller section of Scripture due to the importance of the topic—the two greatest commandments. When these interactions are concluded, Jesus will not speak again to the religious leaders until his arrest in the garden (Mark 14:43–52).

Digging In

A scribe, overhearing Jesus' answers and recognizing his wisdom, asked him, "Which command is the most important of all?"[13] The Law (Torah, Genesis through Deuteronomy) contains 613 separate commands, and Jewish leaders frequently argued about which of them were more important than others. While no commandment of God is unimportant, some were recognized as more significant than others.

Jesus' reply combined two commands from the Law. The first, Deuteronomy 6:4–5, was probably the best-known verse in the Old Testament. Faithful Jews repeated this command twice a day. The passage is called "the Shema" because it begins with the Hebrew word translated "listen." The greatest commandment corresponds to the first part of the Ten Commandments (Exod. 20:2–11), which deals with a person's relationship to God. The oneness of God is foundational to Jewish and Christian monotheism and is the basis for the command to love God with all one's heart, soul, mind, and strength; that is with one's entire being and is a call to wholehearted devotion.

The second great command is from Leviticus 19:18 and corresponds to the second part of the Ten Commandments (Exod. 20:12–17), which concerns a person's relationship with others. The words "as yourself" mean to love others just as much as you love yourself. This, however, is not a call to some sort of self-centered love. Jesus has already taught the disciples that we should be the "servant of all" (Mark 9:35; 10:43–44). The point is that everyone cares for themselves and their physical and emotional well-being. We should love others with the same consideration we extend to ourselves.[14]

The two commands are not independent but are intricately related as one command. Their integration precludes a spiritual life that is concerned only with one's own spiritual growth and life on the one hand and on the other hand, one that may be concerned only with serving and meeting the needs of others. God demands that we be serious about our relationship with him and that the relationship be worked out in serving others.

The scribe's response, that loving God and neighbor is more important than all offerings and sacrifices, emphasizes the foundational nature of these two commandments. This same attitude can be found in the Old Testament as well; for example, 1 Samuel 15:22, "to obey is better than sacrifice," and Hosea 6:6, "I desire faithful love and not sacrifice." The thought is that while sacrifices are essential, the sacrifices of the heart are even more essential. The account concludes with Jesus commending the scribe.

Living It Out

We are not told the fate of this man. Jesus tells him that he is not far from the kingdom. Mark may have left the question open as to the man's salvation so that the readers would ask the question of themselves: "Have I entered the kingdom of God?" More importantly, Jesus summarizes for us what heartfelt religion looks like: a wholehearted love for God and a love for other people. Our religion, if it is honoring to God, should cause our thoughts to be saturated with God's Word, our affections and desires to manifest a burning passion for God's glory, a lifestyle of service to God's people and an evangelistic zeal for the lost. Western Christianity is characterized, to a great degree, by lethargy and the casualness that fails to exhibit the transforming power of the new birth. So, today, let us love God wholeheartedly and love people in a way that glorifies him!

A Study in Contrasts

Mark 12:35–44

The Big Picture

These events take place in the hours before Jesus leaves Jerusalem on Tuesday of Passion Week. The previous passage concluded: "And no one dared to question him any longer." Jesus now asks a question that delights the large crowd (Mark 12:35–37). After answering the question, he moves on to contrast the hypocrisy of the scribes with the wholehearted devotion of a widow (12:38–44). As you study the passage, notice the contrast between the person of Jesus and the scribes and the difference between the scribes and the impoverished widow.

Digging In

Jesus asks the final question of the day. If they want to know who Jesus believes himself to be, he spells it out for them here. Jesus asks a rhetorical question: "How can the scribes say that the Messiah is the son of David?" He answers the question himself by referring to Psalm 110:1. He affirms Davidic authorship of the Psalm and attributes David's words to the inspiration of the Holy Spirit.

Jesus then asks the logical question that has dramatic implications: "David himself calls him 'Lord'; how then can he be his son?" As the most frequently quoted Old Testament verse in the New Testament, Psalm 110:1 is quoted or alluded to some thirty-three times. A coronation Psalm, Psalm 110 was read when a king was installed. Jesus quotes this first verse, not to deny that he is the Davidic Messiah, but to affirm that he is more than the Davidic Messiah—he is a descendant of David and, at the same time, David's God (cf. 2 Sam. 7:12–13).[15] So, Jesus is more than the long-awaited Messiah: he is indeed the Son of God (1:1, 11; 3:11; 5:7; 9:7; 14:61–62; 15:39).

Psalm 110 becomes the dominant proof-text for the exaltation of Jesus in the early church (cf. Acts 2:33–35; Rom. 8:34; 1 Cor. 15:25; Col. 3:1; Heb. 1:3, 13). For Jesus to be seated at the right hand is a way of saying that he is in the position of power and glory and acknowledges that Jesus will be victorious over his enemies, even though, at this moment, things look ominous. From beginning to end, the Old Testament exudes an expectation that someone is coming!

Jesus now turns his attention to the scribes (12:38–44). By arranging the stories as he does, Mark contrasts Jesus (Messiah and Incarnate Lord) and the religious teachers (arrogant and hypocritical) and the widow (wholeheartedly devoted). Jesus is disgusted by the hypocrisy of the scribes. When you compare Mark's condemnation of the religious leaders to Matthew (23:1–36), Mark has greatly abbreviated a longer denunciation.

Jesus brings three charges against them. First, they were selfishly ambitious. They looked for honor from men rather than from God (cf John 5:44; 12:43), which is why they walked around in long robes and yearned for respectful greetings in the marketplaces. They demonstrated little concern for those they taught and were called to shepherd. Second, they were arrogant. They loved to have the best seats and sit at tables with the most prominent of people. Whether in a religious setting or in secular life, they always desired the pride of being placed with the most important people. Jesus' approach was so different. He came to minister and serve those on the fringes of society. Third, they were greedy. They preyed on the most vulnerable. In such few words, Jesus lays bare their crooked hearts. His final words to the religious leaders were a warning of great condemnation.

In the final verses of the chapter, Jesus is impressed by the sacrificial giving of an unnamed widow (12:41–44). Mark indicates that Jesus strategically situated himself so he could watch as people gave their offerings. The event takes place in the Court of the Women. He describes Jesus observing how the rich were putting large amounts of money into the temple treasury. There were thirteen chests used to collect the temple tax as well as freewill offerings. As he watches the rich putting in large sums, he makes no comment of commendation; however, a widow putting in all she had to live on catches his attention.

Widows were some of the most vulnerable people in the ancient world. Normally, a man's estate went first to his sons and the wife was to be cared for by the family. The two small coins were worth 1/64 of a denarius. So, her offering would have barely been enough to buy her a very modest amount of food for a single meal. The point was that from a worldly perspective her offering was inconsequential.

Jesus was so impressed by her faith that he calls the disciples together to seize upon a teachable moment. Jesus' use of "truly" suggests the significance of the moment. She stands in contrast to the Rich Young Ruler (10:17–31). The key lesson on giving learned from this impoverished woman is that one's giving is not measured by amount, but by sacrifice.

Living It Out

So, what does this passage mean for us living in the twenty-first century? First, education and theological sophistication is not the same thing as character. Paul warned us of the danger of knowledge making us proud (1 Cor. 8:1). Whenever our knowledge leads us to become hyper-critical, we are in danger of becoming like these religious leaders. However, we should not misunderstand Jesus to be saying that we should avoid learning and growing in our faith. In fact, the truth is instrumental to spiritual growth. The key is to make sure that we grow in knowledge, love, and devotion to Jesus, seeking to serve others rather than being served. A final thought has to do with a statement attributed to Jesus in the book of Acts but not found in the Gospels: "It is more blessed to give than to receive" (Acts 20:35). This thought is beautifully exemplified in the sacrificial giving of this unnamed widow.

Jesus Predicts the Destruction of the Temple

Mark 13:1–13

The Big Picture

The lengthy discourse of chapter 13 is known as the Olivet Discourse or the Eschatological Discourse, which develops further an important theme of Passion Week: God's judgment of the nation. This theme has been seen in the cursing of the fruitless fig tree (Mark 11:12–14, 20–21), the cleansing of the temple (11:15–19), Jesus' harsh condemnation of the religious leaders depicted in the parable of the vineyard (12:1–12), and his stern rebuke of the scribes (12:38–40). Jesus made abundantly clear that divine judgment was coming!

Chapter 13 can be divided into three major sections. After an introductory section containing two questions (13:1–4), Jesus prophesies the destruction of the temple. He then adds a list of events that should not be mistakenly thought of as immediately preceding the destruction (13:5–13).

He then proceeds to describe events leading to the destruction of Jerusalem. These events foreshadow events prior to and culminating in Jesus' second coming (13:14–27). The discourse concludes with a call for watchfulness in light of the unknown timing of Jesus' coming (13:28–37). Thus, this chapter includes two disturbing prophecies: the destruction of the temple and the end of the world.

Digging In

After spending a day in theological debate with the religious leaders, Jesus leaves the temple for the short walk back to Bethany. The disciples are impressed with the beauty of the temple. Even though they have seen the temple many times they are still astonished by it. The Jerusalem Temple was the largest temple complex in the ancient world. With its white stones, gold trim, and gold-covered roof, the temple complex glistened in the sunlight.

Jesus' reply to the disciples is stunning (13:1–2). This glorious and massive temple complex—a symbol of strength, permanence, and God's favor for the Jews—would be totally destroyed. The fact that not one stone would be left on top of another emphasized the total devastation that would result from Rome's systematic attack on Jerusalem and especially the temple complex.

They would have exited the city through the Eastern gate, crossed the Kidron Valley and walked up the western slope of the Mount of Olives overlooking the city (13:3). Jesus' first four followers question him about his comments concerning the temple. Matthew's Gospel makes clear that their questions have to do with both the destruction of the temple (and Jerusalem) and his Second Coming (Matt. 24:1–4). They possibly thought that the two would happen simultaneously.

Jesus makes a helpful clarification indicating that there will be some preliminary events that do not signal the end (13:5–13). He warns them ("Watch out") about the danger of deception; specifically, about people claiming to be the Jewish messiah. Jesus then lists a series of natural and moral disasters that people often wrongly associate with the end (13:7–8). Jesus' use of the Greek term translated "must" indicates God's sovereignty over these events. Jesus says, "It is not yet the end" and "These are the beginning of birth pains." But just as birth pains precede childbirth, God's judgment would inevitably follow.

Jesus now tells his disciples to "be on your guard" concerning coming persecution (13:9). He does not want them to be caught off guard when persecution comes. This persecution will be both religious and governmental. We need only to read the book of Acts to see how quickly Jesus' words came to pass.[16] He then adds, "it is necessary that the gospel be preached to all nations" (13:10). Despite tremendous persecution, the gospel ("good news") will be proclaimed throughout the world and was to take place before the destruction of Jerusalem. Paul understood the gospel to have been proclaimed throughout the world in his day (Rom. 16:26; Col. 1:6, 23).[17]

The disciples are encouraged not to fear when they will experience persecution. The Spirit will help them defend their faith. The world's hatred of Christianity will be so intense that family members will betray family members, even to the point of execution. Ultimately, the world's hatred is the result of its hatred toward Jesus and is expressed in the persecution of his people (John 15:18–16:4). Although this hatred will be worldwide, those who will endure to the end demonstrate their genuine faith in Christ (v. 13).

Living It Out

We must not miss the fact that Jesus is not impressed with buildings. Buildings that matter so much to us, don't matter that much to Jesus. We should understand our facilities as a means to an end but not the end. We often think the building is the church rather than the people. What Jesus was concerned about in the first century is the same thing he is concerned about in the twenty-first century—the people inside the building.

The Destruction of Jerusalem and the Return of Christ

Mark 13:14–27

The Big Picture

The central section of Mark 13 is very difficult. Bible scholars differ on their understanding. I think two things are going on here. First, Jesus is describing the destruction of Jerusalem (answering the disciples' first question). Second, the devastating destruction of Jerusalem foreshadows events at the end of human history (answering the disciples' second question).

Digging In

In verses 14–19, the fall of Jerusalem and the destruction of the temple foreshadow the final days of human history. The phrase "abomination of desolation" has caused no small amount of controversy. The phrase is found three times in Daniel.

> "He will make a firm covenant with many for one week, but in the middle of the week he will put a stop to sacrifice and offering. And the abomination of desolation will be on a wing of the temple until the decreed destruction is poured out on the desolator." (Dan. 9:27)

> "His forces will rise up and desecrate the temple fortress. They will abolish the regular sacrifice and set up the abomination of desolation." (Dan. 11:31)

> "From the time the daily sacrifice is abolished and the abomination of desolation is set up, there will be 1,290 days." (Dan. 12:11)

The prophecies in Daniel pointed first to 167 BC when the Syrian King, Antiochus Epiphanes, desecrated the temple by sacrificing a pig on the altar. Jesus' prophecy picks up on Daniel and points to Titus's entry into the temple during the siege on Jerusalem in AD 70 and then, beyond that event, to the final enemy of God, the Antichrist (2 Thess. 2:1–11; Rev. 13:1–8). Mark inserts a parenthetical warning to his readers to be wise and careful in reading this material (Mark 13:14a).

Jesus gives five examples of the desperate situation that would take place in AD 70 (13:14b–17). First, those who are able to flee the city should run to the mountains to seek refuge. Second, when the time to flee arrives, no one should seek to collect their possessions before fleeing. Third, those in the fields must not return to their homes. Fourth, he warns of the extreme difficulty for those who are pregnant or for those with little children. Fifth, pray that the destruction does not take place in the winter when survival in the mountains will be very difficult while hiding from the Romans.

While the fall of Jerusalem and the destruction of the temple are on the horizon, Jesus' words point beyond these events to the Great Tribulation (13:19; cf. Rev. 7:14). The language is so intense that Jesus is likely speaking to a time beyond the fall of Jerusalem and to the final days of human history culminating in his return. If God does not cut short those days, no one will survive, but God will cut them short because of his elect (13:20). The tribulation God's people will experience at the end of history is so severe that apart from Christ's return no one would survive. Notice that those who are suffering are called God's elect. They are God's people, and yet they suffer at the hands of God's enemies.

Just as in the days leading up to the fall of Jerusalem, God's people have to be careful not to be deceived in the days leading up to his return (13:21–23). Notice the reference to false signs and wonders. Paul instructed the Thessalonian believers,

> The coming of the lawless one is based on Satan's working, with all kinds of false miracles, signs, and wonders, and with every wicked deception among those who are perishing. They perish because they did not accept the love of the truth and so be saved. For this reason God sends them a strong delusion so that they will believe the lie, so that all will be condemned—those who did not believe the truth but delighted in unrighteousness. (2 Thess. 2:9–12; cf. Rev. 13:13–14; 16:14)

Mark now describes, in the briefest of terms, Christ's second coming (13:24–27). Jesus warns that "after that tribulation" (the one just described), there will be signs of cosmic upheaval, which should be contrasted with the earlier reference to natural upheavals of earthquakes and famines. Jesus quotes from Daniel to describe his glorious return (v. 26; Dan. 7:13–14). He will refer to this event described in Daniel again when questioned by the high priest (cf. 14:61–62). Jesus will descend from heaven and gather together his people from one end of the earth to the other.

Living It Out

We should consider three thoughts from today's passage. First, we need to consider the accuracy of Jesus' prophecy concerning the destruction of Jerusalem. Forty years after Jesus made this prediction, the Romans devastated Jerusalem. Jesus was truly a prophet, but he was even more than a prophet. We can certainly trust Christ and his Word.

Second, the differences between Jesus' first and second comings are monumental. He came the first time in weakness, as a defenseless baby. He was surrounded only by his parents and stable animals, an unremarkable beginning for God's Son. In contrast, his second coming will be preceded by cataclysmic prophetic signs—the darkening of the sun, stars falling from the sky, and the powers in the heavens shaken. He will not be hidden away among the animals lying in a manger, but will be accompanied by the angels, descending in the clouds with great glory. When he comes again everyone will see him. What a difference between his two comings!

Finally, believers do not live in fear of those days but with great expectation. While our Lord paints a dark picture of the events preceding his coming, we should not fail to notice that the first thing he will do is to send forth his angels to gather his elect from the four corners of the earth. Notice that God will have his people scattered from one end of the earth to the other. As his gospel spreads, God's children are spread throughout the earth. In addition, let us never forget that Christ Jesus is coming for his people at the end of the ages. In that thought we can truly rejoice!

Be Ready!

Mark 13:28–37

The Big Picture

Jesus moves on from the events of the eschaton to the absolute necessity of vigilance and readiness on the part of his followers. He has spoken of the destruction of Jerusalem and the final days of human history in verses 1–27 and now concludes his teaching on these topics. The extended metaphor of the fig tree in verses 28–31 centers on the destruction of Jerusalem but includes the Second Coming as well. The sayings in verses 32–37 relate specifically to Christ's Second Coming.

Digging In

In verses 28–31, we have the parable of the fig followed by two brief sayings in verses 30–31. The Mount of Olives had both olive trees and fig trees. Jesus points to one of these fig trees to teach the importance of watchfulness and preparation. A fig tree had an early green fig that appeared in March/April and then a fully ripe fig in May. Jesus refers to the sight of the early figs as a sign that fully ripe figs will soon appear. A ripe fig has not yet arrived, but its arrival is near.

Jesus applies the parable to the current discussion. As we have seen throughout chapter 13, Jesus combines the fall of Jerusalem with the foreshadowing of the great tribulation in the final days. This foreshadowing is likely how we should understand this verse and the next. If we are correct in seeing Jesus as intentionally blending these two events, then the same can likely be said of verse 30. The generation living during the ministry of Jesus would be alive when Jerusalem falls in AD 70, but beyond that, when the events of history begin to unfold in the final days, the generation that is alive at that time will be the final generation of human history.

In a world destined for destruction, the disciples' only hope is to place their faith in God and his Word. Notice that Jesus refers to "my words," which include all he has said in chapter 13, but even beyond that, to all he has said to his disciples (Mark 13:31). Jesus' words are eternal; his teachings are more enduring than the fundamental elements of creation. The basic elements of creation will pass away (Ps. 102:26; 2 Pet. 3:7, 10, 12), but his words will never pass away. Isaiah stated in 51:6:

> Look up to the heavens,
> and look at the earth beneath;
> for the heavens will vanish like smoke,
> the earth will wear out like a garment,
> and its inhabitants will die like gnats.
> But my salvation will last forever,
> and my righteousness will never be shattered.

When we read verses like Mark 13:32 ("Now concerning that day or hour no one knows—neither the angels in heaven nor the Son—but only the Father"), we need to remember that Jesus was fully God and fully man. We should not forget that the main point Jesus is making is the importance of being ready. If the Son himself did not know the day or hour, Christians should keep from seeking such knowledge for themselves.

Verses 33–37 contain three variations of the same basic warning. The repetition emphasizes the need for vigilance. The point of the parable of the man going on a long journey suggests that Jesus' return would not be soon in regard to his original hearers. God's people are to remain busy until Jesus returns. Waiting on Christ does not encourage idleness but service. The four periods of the night correspond to the Roman division of the night into four watches of three hours each and simply mean that the master can return at any time during the night.

Living It Out

We should be looking with great anticipation to the day of Christ's appearing (Titus 2:13; 1 Cor. 16:22; 2 Tim. 4:8; Rev. 22:20). While the precise time of Jesus' return is purposely withheld from us, the event itself is certain. Paul exhorted the Thessalonian believers, "Let us not sleep, like the rest, but let us stay awake and be self-controlled" (1 Thess. 5:6).

Devotion and Treachery

Mark 14:1–11

The Big Picture

This section moves us into the final days of Passion Week. Passover was celebrated on Thursday night in the Jewish month of Nisan. The Feast of Unleavened Bread was observed the following seven days. In this section, Mark brings together those who will be most responsible for the betrayal and arrest of Jesus. They have wanted to arrest him often but have failed time and time again. Judas, one of the Twelve, will provide them with the necessary information to arrest Jesus. In contrast, we find an unnamed woman whose extravagance is in stark contrast to both the religious leaders and Judas. This is a simple story with powerful and important lessons to be learned.

Digging In

These opening verses depict the dark side of unconverted religion (Mark 14:1–2). Two days before the Passover, which begins Thursday night, the religious leaders were plotting to arrest Jesus. The chief priests controlled the temple while the scribes controlled the synagogues. Together, they were formidable foes to Jesus. Yet, they feared the crowds because of Jesus' popularity. They had wanted Jesus dead for some time.

Mark now describes an event that happened earlier in the week while Jesus was in Bethany (14:3–9). This event is told by Matthew, Mark, and John, but it is only John who gives us the specific time when it occurred. He mentions that the anointing took place six days before the Passover (John 12:1). Mark tells us that two days before the Passover the leaders were plotting against Jesus.

Mark wants to contrast this woman, who anoints Jesus, with the religious leaders who want to kill him (1–2) and Judas who will betray him (10–11). Mark sets up this section in an A/B/A pattern ("Markan sandwich") to highlight this contrast. On the outside, there are those plotting against Jesus—the leaders and Judas—and in between this unnamed woman. Only John's gospel identifies her as Mary of Bethany.

The location of the celebratory dinner is in the home of Simon the leper. We know nothing else of this individual other than he was likely one of the many that Jesus must have healed. The fact that they were reclining at the table along with the woman's anointing suggests this meal was special. The woman is described as coming with an alabaster vial of very costly perfume. The value of the perfume was three hundred denarii, which was equal to a year's wage for a common laborer. The exorbitant worth of the perfume is due to the fact that it was extracted from the root of a plant grown in India. Mark indicates the alabaster was "pure nard."

The vial may have been a family heirloom. In verses 4–5, we see the disciples' shocking critique of her. Their response is stunning for the readers of the Gospel. John tells us that Judas was the primary spokesperson, but clearly the other disciples fell quickly into place (John 12:4). These men loved Jesus, but their hearts easily criticized one who was willing to demonstrate extravagant devotion to him.

Jesus defends her and then answers their criticism. She held nothing back in her love for him. Jesus' words concerning the poor are occasionally misunderstood to mean that he did not care about the poor. In fact, he is saying just the opposite. His point is that, at such a seminal moment in redemptive history, her act is so significant that it is entirely appropriate for her to extravagantly anoint him.

He then interprets her act and its significance. She is preparing him for his burial. Did Mary understand herself to be doing this? She probably did not understand what she did in this way. Her act of devotion meant more to Jesus than she could have ever imagined. In this very festive moment, Jesus' mind is on the cross. Jesus goes on to predict that her act will be remembered throughout the ages.

Judas's response gives us insight into his character. Apparently, this event and Jesus' rebuke may have caused him to sell Jesus out to the religious leaders. John tells us that Judas had no concern for the poor but was himself a thief (John 12:6). How interesting that they gave him money in exchange for information (v. 11). Matthew indicates that Judas himself asks what they would give him in return for information on how to arrest Jesus (Matt. 26:15).

Earlier in his ministry, Jesus asked the penetrating question, "What can anyone give in exchange for his life?" (Mark 8:37). Let these verses be a somber warning to every person—nothing is worth having if you lose Jesus. Judas may be an example of one on whom the seed was sown among the thorns; "these are the ones who hear the word, but the worries of this age, and the deceitfulness of wealth, and the desires for other things enter in and choke the word, and it becomes unfruitful" (4:18–19).

Living It Out

I want us to reflect for a moment on the magnificent example in Mary of Bethany of wholehearted devotion. She is a striking contrast to what passes today as Christianity. Her love for Jesus stands out as odd and overboard for those who have a "casual" relationship to Christ. Too many are content with a rather bland and minimalist devotion to Jesus. They are happy to be identified with Jesus but aren't interested in making sacrifices for kingdom advancement.

Let us follow Mary's example of holding nothing back in our devotion to Jesus. We will never regret expressions of unrestrained love and devotion toward Jesus. But, we may one day regret opportunities we missed because we played things too close to the vest. The words of Isaac Watts are an apt conclusion to this narrative:

> Were the whole realm of nature mine, That were a present far too small; Love so amazing, so divine, Demands my soul, my life, my all.

Preparations for Passover

Mark 14:12–21

The Big Picture

The unnamed woman's act of worship by anointing Jesus for burial leads to the Last Supper, which explains the significance of his atoning death. Jesus' prophecy of his coming betrayal shows his awareness of what is taking place. He was not caught off guard by Judas's act. The passage describes how Jesus made meticulous plans to eat the Passover meal with his disciples. One of the most important theological points made in this section is that Jesus unites the Last Supper with the Passover meal.

Digging In

Mark describes in verses 12–16 preparations for the Passover meal. The connection between the Last Supper and the Passover meal is indicated by repeated references to the Passover (Mark 14:12, 14, 16). Passover was a pilgrimage festival for the Jews. Because of this, the city would have been filled with thousands of people. Passover falls in March or April each year.

Jesus' instructions to the disciples are similar to those in preparation for the Triumphal Entry. The careful preparations made for this meal stress its importance to Jesus. Sometimes the Passover was referred to in conjunction with the Feast of Unleavened Bread, which officially began the day after Passover. Since the city would have been filled with tens of thousands of pilgrims, finding a location in advance was essential.

Jesus instructs two of his disciples to make preparations for them and informs them how to find the location. They would be led there by meeting a man carrying a jar of water. The disciples were to follow him and were given the words to speak to the owner of the house. There they would find a large upper room, furnished and made ready for them. The disciples entered the crowded city, and everything unfolded just as Jesus said.

It was not by chance but by God's providential appointment, Jesus was crucified during the Passover week. The Passover commemorated the most important event in Israel's history—God's miraculous deliverance of the people of Israel from Egyptian bondage.

At the time of the exodus from Egypt, each family was to slaughter a lamb and spread the lamb's blood on the door posts. Then, when the death angel passed through the country, he would bypass those who obeyed God's command. Every year, they would commemorate God's deliverance and were inspired to trust God for another great act of deliverance when the Messiah would come.

The preparations for the Passover meal included: a lamb which had to be slaughtered, cleaned, and roasted over an open fire; a bowl of salt-water; bitter herbs; unleavened bread; and a bowl of fruit puree. Enough wine for each person to drink four cups reminded the participants of the four promises in Exodus 6:6–7.

In verses 17–21, Mark describes the betrayal of Judas. The readers would be reminded of how far one can go in religion and still not be saved. The Passover meal would have been eaten in a reclining position, as were other banquet meals. During the Passover meal, someone (usually the youngest son) would ask the host, "Why is this night different from other nights?" The father, or host, would then recount the stories of the Passover and the Exodus (Deut. 26:5–9).

The elements of the Passover meal are symbolic. The Passover lamb served as a reminder of the blood of the sacrificial lambs that protected Israelite homes from the death angel, which visited the firstborn in Egypt (Exod. 12:28–30). The saltwater symbolized the bitter tears of their bondage. The unleavened bread recalled their swift exodus from Egypt (Exod. 12:31–34, 39). The bitter herbs reminded them of their slavery, and the fruit puree reminded them of the clay used to make bricks during their bondage in Egypt. The four cups of wine acknowledged God's fourfold promise in Exodus 6:6–7.

> "Therefore tell the Israelites: I am the LORD, and I will bring you out from the forced labor of the Egyptians and rescue you from slavery to them. I will redeem you with an outstretched arm and great acts of judgment. I will take you as my people, and I will be your God. You will know that I am the LORD your God, who brought you out from the forced labor of the Egyptians."

As the meal begins, Jesus announces that one of them is a traitor. The horrific act of betrayal was more heinous in that the traitor was one of those eating with them (Ps. 41:9). The solemnity of the announcement is seen in his use of "truly" (Mark 14:18). The disciples are stunned and brokenhearted at Jesus' words. They ask, "Surely not I?"

For the first time, they hear of Jesus' betrayal; however, Mark's readers have known since 3:19. Interestingly enough, Jesus did not tell them specifically that Judas is the traitor. He does, however, tell them that it will be one of them, the one who would dip bread in the bowl with him.

The betrayal is both the fulfillment of God's plan, having been prophesied in Scripture and predicted by Jesus, but also the willful choice of the traitor. Neither Jesus, nor the gospel writers, explains how God's sovereignty and Judas's human responsibility can coexist, but both are stated without embarrassment. That Jesus must die according to the Scriptures may be a reference to passages such as Isaiah

52:13–53:12. The "woe" pronounced by Jesus is used in prophetic judgment oracles (Isa. 10:5; Jer. 23:1). The emphasis is on the certainty of Judas's punishment.

Living It Out

I want us to consider two thoughts from this passage. First, things are not always as they appear to be. A detached observer would think that Satan was having his way and winning the war, but God was in absolute control of the events transpiring. Often in our darkest moments we find God doing his greatest work in us and for us. Second, the uniting of the Passover and the Lord's Supper indicates that Jesus will die as God's Lamb to provide a means for his people to be set free from bondage to Satan and sin.

Jesus' Body and Blood

Mark 14:22–31

The Big Picture

The Lord's Supper focuses our attention directly on Jesus Christ's person and work—in many ways a window into the cross-work of Christ. This passage takes us into the Upper Room as Jesus inaugurates the Lord's Supper, a personal moment between Jesus and his disciples. While they fail to grasp the importance of the events at this time, they later come to understand the significance of the new covenant sealed with Jesus' blood.

Digging In

The meal would have begun with a prayer, blessing God for his provision, "Blessed are you, O Lord our God, King of the universe, who brings forth bread from the earth." Mark describes the eating of the bread and the drinking of the wine in verses 22–26.

Jesus takes the bread and gives it to the disciples saying, "Take it; this is my body." Jesus then "took a cup, and after giving thanks, he gave it to them, and they all drank from it. He said to them, 'This is my blood of the covenant, which is poured out for many.'" The bread represents Jesus' body to be broken and the wine represents his blood, poured out on behalf of sinners.

In Mark, Jesus focuses on the cup. The cup of wine represents Jesus' blood, poured out as a sacrifice. Normally, each person participating in the Passover meal had their own cup. Here, Jesus emphasizes the unity of the community by having each one drink from the same cup. The cup represents the establishment of the (new) covenant between God and his people (Luke 22:20; 1 Cor. 11:25).[18] The prophet Jeremiah spoke of this new covenant.

> "Look, the days are coming"—this is the LORD's declaration—"when I will make a new covenant with the house of Israel and with the house of Judah. This one will not be like the covenant I made with their ancestors on the day I took them by the hand to lead them out of the land of Egypt—my covenant that they broke even though I am their master"—the LORD's declaration. "Instead, this is the covenant I will make with the house of Israel after those days"—the LORD's declaration. "I will put my teaching within them and write it on their hearts. I will be their God, and they will be my people." (Jer. 31:31–33)

Jesus' use of "truly" signifies the importance of his statement that he will not drink of "the fruit of the vine" until the day he drinks it new in the kingdom of God, suggesting God's plan for mankind will not be complete until Christ's return. Jesus will not drink the fruit of the vine again until he drinks it at the messianic banquet in Revelation 19:6–8. Each time believers celebrate the Lord's Supper, they look forward to this eschatological banquet.

They concluded their time together by singing the latter part of the Hallel Psalms (Pss. 114–118). After leaving the Upper Room, they cross the Kidron Valley on their way to the Garden of Gethsemane. The discussion in Mark 14:27–31 likely takes place on the way. Jesus has already predicted the betrayal of Judas, which will be fulfilled in 14:43–45. Now he predicts that all of them "will fall away," which will be fulfilled in 14:50–52. This abandonment fulfills Zechariah 13:7, "Strike the shepherd and the sheep will be scattered." The reference to Zechariah 13:7 suggests Jesus' death is part of God's plan and demonstrates his sovereign control over what is about to transpire.

The verb translated "scattered" or "fall away" (Mark 14:27) has been used earlier in Mark and denotes serious spiritual failure (4:17; 14:29). The disciples will desert Jesus completely. Jesus continues as he promises that after he has been raised from the dead, he will go before them into Galilee. This statement is repeated by the angel to the women at the empty tomb in 16:7.

Peter insists that he would not fall away. Jesus' use of the word, "truly," places special emphasis on his response. This is the fourth usage of the term in this chapter (vv. 9, 18, 25, 30). Jesus prophesies that before the rooster crows twice Peter will deny him three times. Jesus' words find fulfillment in 14:66–72. Jesus knows exactly what will transpire. Peter keeps insisting that he would die before he ever fell away. He was not alone in his audacity as the others made the same promise.

Living It Out

This passage is filled with important truths for believers. First, the principal object of the Lord's Supper is to remind us of Christ's sacrifice for us on the cross. The bread and wine teach us how sinful sin must be, if nothing but Christ's death could atone for it. Jesus truly is our Passover Lamb.[19] The words of the old hymn are powerfully true, "What can wash away my sin? Nothing but the blood of Jesus."[20]

Second, when a church has the Lord's Supper, they are thinking in several different directions. First, they look back to Christ's cross-work and sacrificial death. Second, they look forward to Christ's Second Coming. Third, they look around to God's graciousness in providing us a Christian family living under the lordship of Christ.

The Darkest Night of All

Mark 14:32–42

The Big Picture

In today's reading, Mark describes an amazing scene depicting Jesus praying with deep anguish, surrounded by his sleeping inner circle, all the while awaiting the arrival of his enemies and his approaching death. Only rarely in the Gospels are we given insight into the inner thoughts of Jesus. The language is stunningly strong and demonstrates a very deep agony of soul.

Digging In

Gethsemane is a garden or orchard on the lower slopes of the Mount of Olives, one of Jesus' favorite places.[21] The name means "oil press." The significance of the moment is signaled by Jesus taking the inner circle with him. Mark presents Jesus' agony in prayer with a shocking boldness: he was "deeply distressed and troubled;" "I am deeply grieved to the point of death;" and "[he] fell to the ground."

What is going on here? We are completely unprepared. Some suggest that Jesus was afraid to die which is ridiculous! If he was afraid to die, he would have never returned to Jerusalem. If he was afraid to die, he would not have confronted the religious leaders over and over again, knowing that they wanted to kill him. Others have said he feared dying before the cross. This is equally unconvincing. Jesus predicted he would die by crucifixion on numerous occasions.

The reason Jesus responds as he does is that he is facing the reality that in a few hours he will bear humanity's sins in his body. He would experience the wrath of his Father. The words he will speak from the cross express the agony he was experiencing, "My God, my God, why have you forsaken me," which was the indescribable experience of feeling forsaken by his Father.

While Mark sets forth the intensity of Jesus' anguish, Jesus encourages the disciples to remain with him and to stay awake. Mark sums up the point of Jesus' prayer, including his submission to his Father's will. ("He went a little farther, fell to the ground, and prayed that if it were possible, the hour might pass from him. And he said, 'Abba, Father! All things are possible for you. Take this cup away from me. Nevertheless, not what I will, but what you will.'") Twice before, Mark noted Jesus alone in prayer, but only now do we actually "hear" his prayer.

He addresses God the Father using an affectionate and reverential address of a Jewish child or an adult to their father—"Abba." Mark translates the term for his readers. Jesus calls God, Father, not on a mountaintop (Mark 9:7), but in the darkness of approaching death.

Christ's affirmation of God's omnipotence ("all things are possible for you"), demonstrates his trust in God's power. His request, that the Father "take this cup away from me" in the context of the gospel as a whole, is a bold and striking prayer. From Caesarea Philippi through the Last Supper, Jesus is clearly determined to drink the cup. As the beloved Son, Jesus does not want to experience the agony of separation, which is a beautiful example of genuine honesty in prayer.

Jesus' submission to the Father's will is not words spoken from an ivory tower theologian, but the words of one who prays with the profound conviction that God's will is always best. Jesus prays for something that God cannot answer affirmatively. Some might say that God

THE DARKEST NIGHT OF ALL

didn't answer Jesus. He did. He just said no. There is not another way. Jesus must drink the cup of God's wrath.[22] Jesus knows God's plan and continues his prayer, "Nevertheless, not what I will, but what you will." These words tap into the deepest current in Jesus' life.

God's answer comes through the events that unfold—betrayal, arrest, abandonment, denial, beatings, trial, mockery, and crucifixion. Jesus must have experienced great disappointment and loneliness in Gethsemane as he prayed while his disciples slept. The disciples' obtuseness throughout the gospel has prepared the reader for this moment. Three times he finds them sleeping.

Jesus' remarks give further insight into the meaning of the scene. The word *temptation* recalls one of the opening scenes in the gospel (cf. 1:12–13). The battle is not simply with death but with the evil one himself. The disciples are "flesh" dominated. They had nothing they could say in their own defense.

The passage comes to a crescendo with three fateful forces coming together: "The time has come"; "The Son of Man is being betrayed"; "My betrayer is near." Jesus instructs the disciples to rise from their slumber. His prayer had steeled his resolve to follow God's plan through to the end. Despite their secret plot, Jesus' opponents have not taken him by surprise.

Living It Out

Jesus' season of intense darkness helps us understand why he is able to comfort us in our hours of great darkness. But more than that, this passage reveals that he has taken the sting from our darkest hour, for he entered our God-forsaken condition so that we can know God's eternal presence. Jesus fortified his soul to withstand the onslaught of fear through a willingness to stand alone in prayer. As disciples, we learn we are never safer than when we embrace God's will, even when we can't see where he's taking us. The means to embrace God's will in tough times and resist the onslaught of temptation through heartfelt prayer. When Jesus found himself in Gethsemane on the night he was betrayed, he prayed. What about you and me?

Jesus' Betrayal and Arrest

Mark 14:43–52

The Big Picture

This scene describes Jesus' arrest in Gethsemane, which is the opportunity the religious leaders have been waiting for. As we have seen, the opportunity has come through Judas's betrayal, one of Jesus' own disciples. Mark's description is brief with a minimum of theological elaboration. The stark horror of the event speaks for itself. The scene fulfills the words of Jesus in Mark 14:27, "All of you will fall away, because it is written: I will strike the shepherd, and the sheep will be scattered."

In addition, we see the difference prayer makes in times of testing. Jesus told the disciples to pray that they may not fall into temptation. Jesus prayed and the disciples slept. Jesus stood strong and courageous. The disciples, however, abandoned their master and fled into the night.

Digging In

Mark ties together the Gethsemane experience and the arrest ("While he was still speaking . . ."). Jesus' previous statement is now confirmed, "Get up; let's go. See, my betrayer is near." Despite the plot of Jesus' enemies, they do not take him by surprise. Judas is clearly identified as "one of the Twelve." The opponents are identified as the religious establishment—the chief priests, the scribes, and the elders. They had stalked him since his actions in the temple (Mark 11:27). The crowd brings swords and clubs, a detail that heightens the atmosphere of violence. They venture into the night armed, as if they are trying to arrest a violent criminal.

The sign of betrayal is a kiss. Mark is terse in his description of this event. The reason that a sign of identification was needed is due to the darkness of the night and to make sure there is no mistake as to which of the men was Jesus. Judas greets Jesus by calling him "Rabbi" and kissing him—a chilling depiction of the betrayal of a friend. A sign of love is transformed into something sinister.

The treacherous use of a kiss is found in other places in the Bible, as in the story of Absalom ingratiating himself to those coming to see David (2 Sam. 15:5) and with Joab's killing of Amara (2 Sam. 20:8–10). The author of Proverbs 27:6 notes, "the kisses of an enemy are excessive."

After the sign is given, the mob moves into action. With few words, Mark describes the Son of Man being "handed over." What took place in this moment is unclear due to the brevity of words. Mark's description is unclear if the culprit who strikes with the sword is a disciple or merely one of the mob, inadvertently cutting off the slave's ear. John, writing his gospel approximately twenty-five to thirty years later, indicates that the slave's name was Malchus and that Peter cut off his ear. While Mark does not describe the healing of the slave's ear, Luke the beloved physician does (Luke 22:51).

Jesus' words in Mark 14:48–49 draw attention to the stark difference between his integrity and the lack of integrity in his opponents. They have come out on Passover evening to arrest him as if he were a common thief. In contrast, he taught openly in the temple courts. His words contrast his bravery with their cowardice.

Jesus understands this horrible moment as fulfilling the Scriptures. What Scriptures Jesus is referring to is difficult to know for certain. Perhaps he is making reference to Isaiah 53 (cf. 14:46–49), or more particularly to Zechariah 13:7, quoted by Jesus in verse 27 and fulfilled, at least in part, at this time. Another approach is to understand "Scriptures" not as a reference to some specific texts in which the moment of arrest is prophesied but to the entire salvific intent of God, which the early church saw woven throughout the Old Testament.

The disciples abandon Jesus in fulfillment of verses 27–31. The literal rendering emphasizes the moment even more—"and leaving him they fled, all of them," which is one of the saddest moments in redemptive history. Jesus is abandoned by his closet friends and arrested like a common criminal. Yet, before we are too critical of the disciples, we must realize that we would have done the exact same thing. This scene of mob violence concludes with a bizarre epilogue describing an unnamed young man fleeing into the night (v. 52).

This event has been interpreted in various ways. Some consider the young man to be a symbolic incident. The term used to describe the young man is identical with that used in 16:5 to describe the figure who greets the women at the empty tomb. The "linen cloth" is the word used to describe Jesus' burial cloth in 15:46. Therefore some suggest that this strange incident in the garden is a symbolic prelude to the resurrection story: as Jesus is arrested, the narrative flashes ahead to the empty tomb story. Jesus will ultimately escape the clutches of death in resurrection, shedding his burial garments as the young man does in the garden. However, this understanding seems highly unlikely since the narrative appears to be a straightforward report of an actual historical event.

Certainly, this incident is intended to communicate the terrible confusion taking place as Jesus is arrested. Although the young man is not identified, the anonymity may suggest that this is John Mark, but there is no way to know this for certain. The fine linen garment may indicate that the youth was from a wealthy family. He escapes naked, which indicates that he dressed hastily to follow Jesus and the disciples to the garden.

Living It Out

Jesus' words have come to pass. The Son of Man is abandoned by all his followers. As Mark's readers, we are compelled to examine the tenacity of our own commitment to Christ. Do we have a tendency to remain silent when opportunities arise for us to speak a word for the gospel? Is our Christianity one that goes with the flow, or does our lifestyle run counter to the prevailing winds of our decaying culture? Mark's readers learn from this passage that following Christ will not always be easy, which is what Jesus meant in part when he said, "If anyone wants to follow after me, let him deny himself, take up his cross, and follow me. For whoever wants to save his life will lose it, but whoever loses his life because of me and the gospel will save it" (Mark 8:34–35).

Jesus before the Sanhedrin

Mark 14:53–65

The Big Picture

The Passion story now has a major change of setting; from the garden, where Jesus was arrested, to the court of the high priest where Jesus will be tried. Jesus is now face-to-face with his enemies. Mark brackets Jesus' trial before the Sanhedrin by a reference to Peter on the one side and a description of Peter's three denials on the other side. This "Markan sandwich" (A/B/A) is intended to highlight the differences between the two.

Digging In

Jesus is taken before the Sanhedrin. Peter follows right into the courtyard of the high priest. Unlike John, Mark does not describe how Peter gained access to the courtyard (John 18:15). As the passage unfolds, Peter drifts into the background and Jesus moves into the foreground.

Verse 55 paints the Sanhedrin as in a panic trying to find witnesses to testify against Jesus. As the proceedings progress, they attempt to muster false witnesses against him. Jewish law stated that at least two, and better three, witnesses had to agree before imposing the death penalty (Num. 35:30; Deut. 17:6; 19:15). One of the major accusations against Jesus is his alleged threats against the temple. They misunderstood something Jesus said almost three years earlier (not found in Mark's Gospel, but in John's). "Destroy this temple [his body], and I will raise it up in three days" [his resurrection] (John 2:19). No matter how hard they tried, they continued to bungle the entire proceedings. We should not be surprised by their lies in light of their hatred of him. Earlier in his ministry, Jesus referred to them as "children of the devil," "the father of lies."

> "You are of your father the devil, and you want to
> carry out your father's desires. He was a murderer
> from the beginning and does not stand in the truth,
> because there is no truth in him. When he tells a lie,
> he speaks from his own nature, because he is a liar
> and the father of lies." (John 8:44)

Jesus' refusal to respond to their false accusation frustrates his interrogators. Jesus' silence ushers the proceedings into the climactic moment of the trial and reminds his readers of Isaiah 53:7.

> "He was oppressed and afflicted,
> yet he did not open his mouth.
> Like a lamb led to the slaughter
> and like a sheep silent before her shearers,
> he did not open his mouth."

The high priest forces the issue and in the most dramatic moment of the trial asks "Are you the Messiah, the Son of the Blessed One?" Jesus responds immediately with "yes" and brings together imagery from Daniel 7:13 (Son of Man, his favorite self-designation) and Psalm 110:1 (Son of God, referred to by Mark in the opening line of the gospel).

"I continued watching in the night visions, and suddenly one like a son of man was coming with the clouds of heaven. He approached the Ancient of Days and was escorted before him. He was given dominion, and glory, and a kingdom; so that those of every people, nation, and language should serve him. His dominion is an everlasting dominion that will not pass away, and his kingdom is one that will not be destroyed." (Dan 7:13–14)

This is the declaration of the LORD to my Lord: "Sit at my right hand until I make your enemies your footstool." (Ps. 110:1)

Jesus' words are dramatic declarations of coming victory. What happens next is nothing less than an expression of undiluted hatred. The high priest tearing off his clothes is a sign of contempt and a judicial act expressing the fact that he regarded Jesus' answer as blasphemous. How Jesus committed blasphemy is not exactly clear. Likely, his words were interpreted as an affront to God's majesty and glory. The trial scene concludes with mockery. These words jolt Mark's reader back to the reality of the moment—the sinless Son of God is on trial for his life—before those committed to killing him.

Living It Out

What can we learn from the example of Jesus here? First, as we reflect on this scene, our hearts should cry out, "Give me Jesus!" What he went through to bring us salvation is almost incomprehensible. Even before he was impaled on the cross, he was arrested like a common criminal as the result of a betrayal by a friend. He was abused and humiliated by the religious leaders. They sought men who would lie about what he said and did. They beat him and taunted him. Finally, they convicted him of blasphemy, which all occurred before they ever handed him over to the Romans. How can we fail to love and serve him with our whole lives for our entire lives? Second, Jesus teaches us how to handle ourselves when unjustly treated.

For you were called to this, because Christ also suffered for you, leaving you an example, that you should
follow in his steps. He did not commit sin, and no
deceit was found in his mouth; when he was insulted,
he did not insult in return; when he suffered, he did
not threaten but entrusted himself to the one who
judges justly. (1 Pet. 2:21–23)

Peter's Denials

Mark 14:66–72

The Big Picture

Mark's focus shifts again; this time to Peter. Mark brackets Jesus' inquisition before the Sanhedrin with references to Peter. While Jesus is being beaten in the home of Caiaphas, Peter is outside in the courtyard with Jesus' enemies. While Jesus confesses his true identity, Peter denies that he knows Jesus. Mark's presentation is masterful as he describes Peter's discipleship going up in smoke, which is the fulfillment of Jesus' earlier prophecy concerning Peter's denials (Mark 14:27–31). Peter had both privilege and ability. He was a gifted man and easy to follow because his strengths were many. But, at the same time, he was stubborn, proud, and overconfident in his own abilities. If God were to use him, there was much work to be done.

Digging In

After Jesus, there is no person in the Gospels referred to as often as Simon Peter. John's Gospel describes his first encounter with Jesus as a result of his introduction by his brother Andrew (John 1:40–42).

In Mark's Gospel, Jesus' first act after his temptation is to call Peter and his brother to leave their fishing business and become his disciple (Mark 1:16–18). Luke describes Peter falling before Jesus after a miraculous catch of fish and crying out "Go away from me, because I'm a sinful man, Lord" (Luke 5:8). Peter is the spokesperson for the Twelve at Caesarea Philippi (8:29). He was on the Mount of Transfiguration with Jesus, James, and John (9:2–9). In the Upper Room, he boldly proclaimed that he would die for Jesus rather than deny him (14:29). Luke alone records the reference to Satan demanding permission to sift Peter (and the other disciples) like wheat (Luke 22:31–34). Jesus went on to tell Peter that he had prayed for him that his faith would not ultimately fail, and he would return and strengthen his brethren (Luke 22:31–32). This scene, however, depicts his sifting.

As the passage unfolds, Mark carefully describes Peter's collapse. Unlike John, Mark does not describe how Peter made his way into the courtyard of the high priest. John's gospel indicates that Peter accompanied another disciple, who knew the high priest, into the courtyard (John 18:15–16). Despite all his shortcomings, entering the courtyard demonstrates Peter's willingness to put himself in a dangerous situation out of love for Jesus. A maidservant of the high priest recognizes Peter as one of Jesus' disciples (Mark 14:66–67). Peter denies understanding, or even knowing, what the servant girl is talking about, and a rooster crows.

Next, she speaks her accusation to others. Again, Peter denies knowing Jesus. Galileans were easily identified by their dialect, and Peter's speech revealed his Galilean origins. Mark's readers would be astonished with the force of Peter's third denial, "Then he started to curse and to swear with an oath, 'I don't know this man you're talking about!'" Just as he finishes his words, a rooster crows. Peter suddenly remembers Jesus' words and collapses in tears. Luke indicates that Jesus turned and looked at Peter at this exact time, and he and Peter locked eyes (Luke 22:61). Here we see the way back. The way back begins with recognition that my sin is abhorrent in Jesus' eyes, costing him his life.

Sometimes the question is asked, "How are Peter's denials different than what Judas did?" On the surface they may seem similar, but in reality, they are very different. Judas is described as being a thief (John

12:6), while Peter is described as having left everything to follow Jesus (Mark 1:16–18). Judas's act of treachery and deceit was premeditated and done out of pure greed (Mark 14:10–11; Matt. 26:14–16). Peter's denials were the result of being overcome by momentary fear for one's life. The major difference is that Peter was overcome by sorrow for what he did and demonstrated repentance by going on to live a life for God's glory and die a martyr's death (John 21:18–19).

Living It Out

We learn from Peter that we are never as strong as we think we are. Peter was not nearly as spiritually mature as he thought he was. Although he was taught by Jesus, he still had a long way to go. What led to his collapse was multifaceted: he was overconfident, proud, refused to listen to Jesus' warning, lacked prayer, and failed to take his own weaknesses seriously.

The impact of this story on Mark's readers is clear. We must beware of the danger of pride. Jesus has taught us the importance of being a humble servant. Yet, like Peter, we are often far too confident in our own strengths, abilities, and wisdom. Self-confidence causes us to depend more on our own ability than on Jesus.

"Suffered under Pontius Pilate"

Mark 15:1–20

The Big Picture

The change in setting and the coming of dawn signal another major change of scene in Mark's passion story. After the transfer to Pilate (Mark 15:1), the passage divides into three brief episodes: an initial interrogation by Pilate (15:2–5); the choice between Jesus and Barabbas (15:6–15); and the mockery of Jesus (15:16–20). In each scene, the issue of Jesus' messianic identity is central.

Digging In

The pace of events quickens noticeably as Mark turns from the Jewish trial to the Roman trial. The opening scene focuses on Pilate seeking to discern if Jesus believes himself to be the king of the Jews (15:1–5). At the break of dawn, the Sanhedrin convenes. The meeting was likely a strategy session. Jesus is led away to be "handed over" (14:10–11; 14:18, 21, 42, 44) to Pilate (v. 1). The third and final passion prediction described the exact sequence of events (10:32–34). The working day of a Roman official began very early. The day is now Friday of Passion week.

Pilate is mentioned without introduction and therefore must have been well known to his readers. He was the fifth Roman procurator of Judea and held office from AD 26–36. Pilate asks Jesus if he is the king of the Jews. The messianic motif had been a major aspect of his Jewish trial. Mark's account of the interrogation is brief, to say the least. Only in 15:16 do we discover that the trial probably took place outside the praetorian.

Jesus' response is somewhat ambiguous "You say so." His answer is clearly less straightforward than the resounding "I am" in 14:62, although not a negative answer. The remainder of the trial recalls the scene before the Sanhedrin. If Jesus offers no defense, then according to Roman law, he will be found guilty (cf. 14:6). Once again, the words of Isaiah ring true,

> He was oppressed and afflicted, yet he did not open
> his mouth. Like a lamb led to the slaughter and like
> a sheep silent before her shearers, he did not open his
> mouth. (Isa. 53:7)

In Mark's Gospel, Jesus' silence remains until the cry of abandonment from the cross. Mark's readers would also think back to the Olivet Discourse and understand that Jesus was the first in a long line who would suffer for the truth (Mark 13:9). Pilate is stunned at Jesus' refusal to defend himself.

The leaders resolve to have Jesus executed comes more clearly into focus in verses 6–15; however, so does the nature of Jesus' royal identity. Mark barely briefs the reader on the custom, which is the type of offer that fits in perfectly with the Passover. Barabbas is identified by his crimes. The name Barabbas means "son of the father." The irony is that the people will choose between Jesus, the beloved Son of God, and one whose name means "son of the father."

Now the crowds begin to turn against Jesus. Up to this point, his primary foes were the religious leaders and Judas. Jesus is being stripped of all support. However, in this early morning trial we must remember that many of those in Jerusalem would just be getting up. The majority of those gathered were likely related to members of the Sanhedrin. The deck is clearly stacked against Jesus.

The crowd enters into direct dialogue with Pilate (15:8–12). Pilate makes a feeble attempt to release Jesus. He refers to him as "King of the Jews." He is aware that the religious leaders are envious of Jesus. Matthew helps us understand that a note from Pilate's wife distracted him long enough for the religious leaders to work the crowd (Matt. 27:19–20). Once again, Jesus is referred to as King of the Jews (cf Mark 15:2, 9).

For the first time, the crowds utter the word, "crucify." Pilate protests, pointing to Jesus' innocence, but again, the crowd cries out for crucifixion (v. 14). In an act of cowardice, Pilate sets Barabbas free and condemns Jesus to be crucified. Jesus is first flogged and then "he [Pilate] handed him over" for crucifixion.

Note the brevity of verse 15; however, what actually took place was an experience of brutality, hideous and gruesome. The criminal was stripped, bound to a post or pillar, sometimes simply thrown to the ground. The instrument was a scourge consisting of leather strips plaited with several pieces of bone or lead. No maximum number of lashes was prescribed by Roman law, and men condemned to flogging frequently died. The flesh commonly was so mutilated that bones or internal muscles and organs might eventually become visible.

There is an interesting contrast here between Jesus and Barabbas. One seeks a kingdom "with swords and clubs" while the other refuses worldly power and seeks to establish a spiritual kingdom. Jesus dies in the place of Barabbas. One who deserves death is set free, while one who does not is condemned as an insurrectionist.

The final scene in this section before the crucifixion brings the motif of Jesus' messianic identity to a profound conclusion (15:16–20). Jesus is led into the governor's residence (praetorian) where he is beaten and abused, the entire time being mocked as a "king."

Pilate's residence was a magnificent palace constructed by Herod the Great, located west and a little south of the temple area. Pilate resided there when he went to Jerusalem. The Roman cohort was stationed in Jerusalem at the palace (praetorium). The cohort was recruited from non-Jewish inhabitants of the Holy Land and assigned to the Roman governor.

Their mocking consisted of Jesus being dressed in purple, having a "crown of thorns" placed on his head, being anointed by the soldiers' spit, and being taunted by false worship. After finishing, they lead him away to crucifixion.

Living It Out

This passage has much to say to us about Jesus. In these verses, Jesus is presented to us as the rejected king. The rejection by the Jewish leaders and crowd are reminiscent of the words of John, "He came to his own, and his own people did not receive him" (John 1:11).

Next, we learn of the destructive power of envy: Pilate knew that the religious leaders were envious of Jesus (Mark 15:10). The difference between envy and jealousy is that envy is the emotion of coveting what someone else has, while jealousy is the emotion related to fear that something you have will be taken away by someone else. Envy begins with empty hands, longing for what one doesn't have. Jealousy is not quite the same. Jealousy begins with full hands but is threatened by the loss of its plenty.

The Crucifixion of the Son of God

Mark 15:21–37

The Big Picture

This passage brings into sharp focus the horror the Son of God experienced to save sinners. The passage consists of three scenes, each marked by the passing of time. First, Jesus is led to Golgotha to the site of crucifixion (Mark 15:21–24). While hanging on the cross, suspended between heaven and earth, the mockery continues (15:25–32). Finally, Jesus' death is depicted (15:33–37). Mark's account focuses on the fact that Jesus dies absolutely alone.

Digging In

Mark's presentation of Jesus' crucifixion is brief and unadorned. The physical torments of the Savior are not described. The likely reason for this omission is that the horrors of crucifixion were well known in the ancient world.

Simon of Cyrene is forced into service to carry Jesus' cross beam. Men condemned to death were usually forced to carry a beam of the cross, often weighing thirty or forty pounds, to the place of crucifixion. The flogging Jesus experienced would have been devastating to his body. Simon was probably in Jerusalem to celebrate Passover. Cyrene was an important city in North Africa and had a large Jewish population. Simon's sons, Alexander and Rufus, are only mentioned by Mark but are referred to in such a way as to suggest that they were known by those to whom Mark wrote. Rufus may be the same person referred to in Romans 16:13.

Golgotha is an Aramaic word which Mark quickly translates for his Greek-speaking readers as "Skull Place," which may have been named for its appearance or because of the many executions that took place there.

The incense was mixed with wine to deaden pain (Mark 15:23). Myrrh is a spice derived from plants native to the Arabian deserts and parts of Africa. Matthew refers to wine and "vinegar" or "gall" (Matt. 27:34), possibly alluding to Psalm 69:21.

Mark adds none of the gruesome details that one would have seen at a crucifixion. He does add a note about the division of Jesus' garments, which seems to be an allusion to Psalm 22:18. Mark will refer again to the psalm.

Crucifixion was a Roman form of execution in which the victim was nailed to a cross. Heavy wrought-iron nails were driven through the wrists and the heel bones. If the life of the victim lingered too long, death was hastened by breaking the legs.

The brief description of the crucifixion gives way to a cascade of verbal abuse. Mark brings into this horrific scene, motifs of Christology and discipleship.

The third hour would have been about 9:00 a.m. We must remember that in an age without watches time was given in estimations. The irony of kingship, so prominent in the trial scene, reappears on the placard placed above Jesus' head. From the vantage point of the reader, the kingly announcement has found the proper place above the head of Jesus.

The two men described as having been crucified with Jesus are described as "rebels" (Isa. 53:12). These two victims add to the mockery inflicted by the soldiers. The fact that Mark describes them as "one on his right and one on his left" reminds the reader of Jesus' reply to James' and John's request to sit on his right and left in his kingdom (Mark 10:40). Mark could very well be reminding his readers that the place of privilege in the kingdom is quite different than the place of power in the world.

Note the repetition of the idea of taunting: "yelling insults" (15:29), "mocking him" (v. 31), and "taunting him" (v. 32). Whether the taunting was by those passing by, the chief priests and the scribes, or the two thieves, all spoke better than they realized. Those passing by make reference to the mistaken idea that Jesus claimed that he would destroy the temple (cf. 14:58). He never made such a claim, though he made a similar statement a couple years earlier recorded in John's Gospel (John 2:19). The repeated taunts that he should save himself and come down from the cross are a failure to understand that if he saved himself there would be no payment for the penalty of sin. As they mock him as Messiah and King, they unknowingly confess his true identity.

The shaking of the heads by those passing by was intended as a taunting gesture and alludes to Psalm 22:7: "Everyone who sees me mocks me; they sneer and shake their heads." No biblical passage is more frequently alluded to in Jesus' suffering on the cross than this psalm, which is close to the surface throughout the entire crucifixion scene.

Mark, more so than Luke and John, highlights Jesus' total abandonment by men. In Luke, one of the two thieves is converted. In John, Jesus' mother and the beloved disciple are nearby. Not so in Mark; Jesus is surrounded only by hostile voices.

This scene is the culmination of Mark's passion narrative beginning with the Triumphal Entry. Mark's description of Jesus' death is in some ways the boldest and most challenging of the four evangelists. Mark supplies another time indicator (12:00 noon until 3:00 p.m.). Mark's reference to the darkness is an allusion to Amos 8:9–10.

Mark seems to understand clearly that Jesus' death had cosmic consequences.

Jesus breaks his silence in Mark 15:34. His last recorded words were in 15:2 before Pilate. Now his words are a quote in Aramaic, which Mark translates for his readers, *"Eloi, Eloi, lemá sabachtháni?"* which is translated, "My God, my God, why have you forsaken me?" His words are the opening line of Psalm 22.

Psalm 22 is a lament psalm, portraying first the desolation of the suffering of the one (vv. 1–21) and then the triumphant vindication of this one by God (vv. 22–31). These are Jesus' final words in this Gospel; abandoned by friends, mocked and tormented by his own religious leaders, surrounded by thieves; he cries out to God. Even his final words are misunderstood and mocked by his enemies (Mark 15:35). The drink should likely be understood as the drink of the soldiers (v. 36). Rather than an act of kindness, the man's words indicate an attitude of mockery.

A debate exists over whether these words are an expression of desolation or faith, despair or trust. There is no reason both cannot be true. The psalm begins with despair but ends with victory. Surely, Jesus felt the isolation of the moment but at the same time he had prayed, "Not what I will, but what you will" (14:36). Mark's description of Jesus' death is raw and stunning (15:37). His presentation is stark with its unadorned brutality.

Living It Out

Jesus, in his seemingly weakest moment, is powerful to save. While Mark does not describe the conversion of one of the two thieves, he does describe Simon in a way that indicates that the readers of the Gospel knew his two sons (Alexander and Rufus). If this is Rufus referred to in Romans 16:13, then it is possible that Simon and his family became believers as a result of his carrying Jesus' cross.

The death of Jesus in Mark's Gospel is a brutal depiction of the extent to which the Son of Man suffered for the salvation of sinners. Abandoned by his followers, taunted by his enemies, and worst of all, forsaken by his Father. This prayer is the only one where Jesus did not address God as Father.

Isaiah 59:1–2 explains why Jesus responded as he did in the garden. He knew that bearing humanity's sins in his body and experiencing the cosmic response of darkness was the Father's will.

At the Cross

Mark 15:38–47

The Big Picture

After Jesus dies, Mark describes a series of unexpected events. The first two appear to happen immediately—the temple veil is torn, and a Roman centurion confesses that Jesus is the Son of God. A new character is introduced at this point. Joseph of Arimathea demonstrates tremendous bravery by requesting to give Jesus' body an honorable burial. Watching from a distance, a group of women carefully observe where Jesus' body is laid.

Digging In

Immediately when Jesus dies, the temple veil is torn from top to bottom. Most understand the torn veil to be the one separating the holy place from the Holy of Holies in the temple. The Holy of Holies was a place of absolute sacredness, which could not be entered except once a year by the high priest on the Day of Atonement. Mark's purpose in referring to this event is more than just historical interest.

One of the major themes in Mark chapters 11–13 has been God's judgment on the temple. In one sense, the temple veil is not "opened" but "split." Beginning in Mark 11, the temple is viewed negatively as a "den of thieves," a fig tree that has no fruit and is controlled by those who convict Jesus of blasphemy.

Yet, in light of the heavens being "torn open" at Jesus' baptism, likely there is more to this event than just a culminating reference to the temple's destruction. At Jesus' baptism, God tore the heavens open, and now at Jesus' death, God tears the temple veil. The veil is torn from top to bottom suggesting God tore it. As mentioned earlier, at Jesus' baptism, he identifies with sinners, and at the cross, he dies for them. The author of Hebrews understood the event theologically to mean that through Christ's death the way into God's presence is open to all God's people.

> Therefore, brothers and sisters, since we have boldness to enter the sanctuary through the blood of Jesus—he has inaugurated for us a new and living way through the curtain (that is, through his flesh)—and since we have a great high priest over the house of God, let us draw near with a true heart in full assurance of faith, our hearts sprinkled clean from an evil conscience and our bodies washed in pure water. (Heb. 10:19–22)

The next event described is an unexpected confession by a Roman centurion. The centurion pronounces the first unqualified confession of Jesus as the Son of God by a human being in the Gospel; the only exception is Mark's opening (1:1). The centurion's confession is triggered by observing how Jesus died. Neither Jesus' power over nature, sickness, demons, or death had penetrated the blindness of those around him. But now, in the ultimate weakness of dying, Jesus is recognized as God's Son.

A number of women are watching from a distance. A Gentile and a group of women—both outsiders—are mentioned as seeing Jesus die. The glaring absence of the names of any disciples is a reminder of their abandonment. The naming of the women helps prepare the way for the discovery of the empty tomb.

Mark begins by noting the time, which is now Friday evening, the day of preparation for the Sabbath. Mark has counted off the passage of time throughout the passion story: Thursday "evening" (14:17); "rooster crowed" (14:72); "morning" on Friday (15:1); and "at three" (15:34). One final time note is still to be announced—"very early in the morning, on the first day of the week" (16:2).

The awesome events of Golgotha are followed by a scene that is subdued and somber, an almost anticlimactic finale to the passion story. Yet, the burial account serves an important role in the passion narrative—confirming the reality of the crucifixion—Jesus is dead.

Joseph of Arimathea is introduced into the story. He is described as a prominent member of the Sanhedrin and waiting for the kingdom of God. Matthew 27:57 and John 19:38 identify him as a disciple indicating that not all those who were a part of the Sanhedrin were opposed to Jesus and favored his execution.

Great courage was required for Joseph to request the dead body of a convicted criminal. Public association with executed criminals involved a genuine risk. Pilate's brief role is to confirm that Jesus is actually dead. Pilate seemed surprised that Jesus died so quickly. The words *dead* and *died* are used Mark 15:44 and then confirmed by the centurion in verse 45.

Mark does not specifically mention the anointing of Jesus' body. In one sense, Jesus' body was anointed earlier in Bethany by an unnamed woman (14:3–9). The tomb was hewn out of rock. Matthew indicates that the tomb belonged to Joseph and that it had never been used (Matt. 27:60). John adds that the tomb was in a garden near the site of the crucifixion (John 19:41).

Two of the Galilean women from the cross watch the burial (Mary Magdalene and Mary the mother of Jesus). The long twenty-four hours of agony has ended—beginning in the Upper Room with predictions of death, denial, desertion, betrayal, and ending with Jesus' body placed in a tomb by a person relatively unknown to the readers.

Living It Out

At the moment of Jesus' death, two extraordinary events took place. First, the temple veil was torn from top to bottom. God's presence, the holiest of all places, is now open to all God's people. No matter one's age, education, or social standing, everyone who belongs to God through Christ can enter into his presence.

Second, we cannot know for certain what the centurion meant when he said, "Truly this man was the Son of God!" (Mark 15:39). We know his words to be absolutely true. Only by divine providence is the solitary confession that Jesus is "God's Son," is spoken at the cross. The words from Isaac Watt's famous hymn, "At the Cross" could never be truer than the moment one recognizes Jesus is God's Son who died for them,

> At the cross, at the cross where
> I first saw the light,
> And the burden of my heart rolled away,
> It was there by faith I received my sight,
> And now I am happy all the day![23]

The Resurrection of Jesus Christ

Mark 16:1–8

The Big Picture

The doctrine in the bodily resurrection of Jesus Christ from the dead is ground zero concerning the truthfulness of the Christian message. If Jesus Christ was not raised bodily from the dead, then Christianity is a false religion. But, as we know, he was raised from the dead and the gospel message is true! We will examine the reliable testimony of Mark's Gospel and then make further comments on the matter of the historical reliability of Jesus' bodily resurrection from the dead.

The resurrection of Jesus is a fitting conclusion to both Mark's passion narrative and the entire Gospel. Mark centers his account on the women's discovery of the empty tomb and the angelic announcement that Jesus is alive.

Digging In

The same group of women who witnessed the death and burial of Jesus now prepare to visit the tomb. The Sabbath was over on Saturday at dusk, so the women likely purchased the spices on Saturday evening for the following day, Sunday. The purpose of the spices (perfumes and fragrant oils) was to offset the terrible stench of decomposition.

That they did not expect to find Jesus alive is evident from the purchase of the spices. His earlier prophecies concerning his resurrection from the dead had continually fallen on deaf ears. Nothing in their actions would lead one to believe that they held out the slightest possible hope that Jesus was alive.

The women departed for the tomb in the dark and arrived just after sunrise. As they approach the tomb, they remember they had not considered how they would remove the large stone protecting the entrance. They certainly did not expect the tomb to be open. God, however, had already taken care of the difficulty. The large stone would likely have been four to six feet in diameter. Mark does not say how the stone had been removed, but Matthew 28:2 says that an angel had done so.

They bend down and enter the small opening, expecting to find Jesus' body on the stone bench, but instead they see a "young man" clothed in a white robe. John's Gospel mentions that there were two angels. Mark apparently focuses on the one that is the more vocal of the two.

The women's startled response is natural in light of the circumstance. The angel calms their fear and gives them a mild rebuke. They came to the tomb looking to anoint a corpse, but Jesus is alive. The angel's reference to Jesus as "the Nazarene," emphasizes the humble origins of the risen Savior. The women were looking for the one "who was crucified," but they should be looking for the one who "has been resurrected." He points to the place were Jesus' body had been laid.

According to the Holman Christian Standard Bible, the angel's words, "He has risen!" may be the most wonderful words in the history of the world! The phrase "he has been resurrected" is a divine passive (literally, "he has been raised"), God raised his beloved Son from the grave. In their incredulity and amazement, the angel asked them to trust their eyes: "see the place where they put him" (Mark 16:6).

In verse 7, the angel tells them to "go" and "tell." Now is time for action. They are to report to the disciples and Peter that they will see Jesus in Galilee, just as he promised them (14:28). Peter is especially highlighted in light of his recent denials. His anguished soul would have needed a special word. In fact, Peter received a personal resurrection appearance (Luke 24:34; 1 Cor. 15:5).

The ending of Mark's dramatic account is somewhat perplexing[24] with the words, "They went out and ran from the tomb, because trembling and astonishment overwhelmed them. And they said nothing to anyone, since they were afraid." Surely, we should understand that they refused to be side-tracked from reporting to the disciples—so they stopped and spoke to no one (Luke 24:5–11; John 20:1–2, 18). The ending of the Gospel may indicate that we are now responsible to announce the good news of the Risen Savior!

Living It Out

The question in the minds of many skeptics is, "Did Jesus really rise from the dead?" The historical evidence for the bodily resurrection of Jesus is overwhelming. I will mention just a few pieces of evidence. First, something miraculous must have happened on Easter Sunday for Jewish Christians to change their day of worship from Saturday to Sunday. Something monumental had to change for a people that had always worshiped on the Jewish Sabbath (Saturday) to begin worshiping on the Lord's Day (Sunday).

Second, the fact that women are described as the first witnesses to the empty tomb, and later to be the first to encounter the risen Lord, goes against everything in first-century Judaism (Matt. 28:8–10; John 20:11–18). If you were making up a story about the resurrection the last people you would make your most important initial witnesses would be women. Women were often not considered reliable witnesses in a court of law.

Third, nothing can explain the widespread number of people who are reported as having seen Jesus alive—as many as five hundred in different places and at different times—unless he truly was alive. Reports from this many people certainly could not be hallucinations or visions.

Fourth, if his body were decomposing in a tomb, why did the Jewish leaders not present the decomposed body to the masses in Jerusalem? All they had to do was to present Jesus' corpse in order to silence the apostles preaching of the resurrection.

Fifth, if the disciples stole Jesus' body, then why would the apostles endure beatings, impoverishment, and martyrdom for something they knew to be a lie? People may suffer and die for something they think to be true, but suffering and dying for something they know is not true makes absolutely no sense.

Finally, something dramatic must have happened to transform the disciples from cowards to courageous martyrs. When the day began, they were in hiding. In a matter of a few weeks, they were preaching courageously to those who crucified Jesus.

The final question that must be asked, "Does Jesus' bodily resurrection from the dead really matter?" According to the apostle Paul, resurrection certainly mattered. He wrote, "And if Christ has not been raised, then our proclamation is in vain, and so is your faith. . . . you are still in your sins! . . . If we have placed our hope in Christ for this life only, we should be pitied more than anyone" (1 Cor. 15:14, 17, 19).

Therefore, if Jesus has been raised from the dead—and he has—then the church has a mandate to take the gospel across the street and around the world. To fail to be concerned about the salvation of others is to diminish the importance of Jesus' death and resurrection.

If one confesses they believe in the resurrection, then they must live a resurrection life. We should build our lives around the things that matter most to God. To say we believe in the resurrection but live a casual form of pseudo-Christianity is to denigrate the person and work of Christ.

If Jesus' death and resurrection could save and transform the apostles, and it did, then Jesus' death and resurrection can save you. To gain the world and not know Jesus is, in the end, to lose everything. But to lose everything for Jesus is, in the end, to gain everything!

Notes

1. The word is used six times in Mark (8:29; 9:41; 12:35; 13:21; 14:61; 15:32).

2. The baptism with the Holy Spirit would fulfill numerous Old Testament promises (Isa. 32:15; 44:3; Ezek. 11:19; 36:26–27; 37:14; Joel 2:28–29).

3. Mark 4:11, 26, 30; 9:1, 47; 10:14, 15, 23, 24, 25; 12:34; 14:25; 15:43

4. See also 8:12; 9:1, 41; 10:15, 29; 11:23; 12:43; 13:30; 14:9, 18, 25, 30. Typically the word *truly* was used by a Jew in response to the words of someone else, to indicate affirmation. Jesus' use as a preface to his own statement is quite unique.

5. See Ezekiel 17:23 and Daniel 4:20–21 which suggest that the image may refer to the Gentiles finding rest in God's kingdom tree.

6. The opposition of the Pharisees was unrelenting 2:16–18, 24; 3:6; 7:1–5; 10:2; 12:13, 15.

7. The word *Gehenna* has a history. In the Old Testament Gehenna was the place where people would sacrifice their children to the false God Molech. In New Testament times Gehenna was a garbage dump where fire continually burned consuming Jerusalem's trash. Gehenna became a picture of the torment of hell.

8. For further study on the topic of marriage and divorce, see Genesis 2:21–25; Matthew 19:1–12; 1 Corinthians 7:10–16; and Ephesians 5:22–33.

9. For other examples of Jesus' supernatural knowledge in Mark's Gospel, see Mark 2:8; 3:5; 5:30, 32; 8:17.

10. Mark has made clear that Jesus is a man of divine authority in his teaching (1:22), to cast out demons (1:26), heal the sick (1:29–2:12), forgive sins (2:10), and to cleanse the temple.

11. See Romans 13:1–7 and 1 Peter 2:13–17 for further insight on the relationship between the believer and government.

12. For references in the resurrection of the dead, see Isaiah 26:19; Ezekiel 37:1–14; Job 19:26; Psalm 16:9–11; 49:15; 73:25–26; and Daniel 12:2.

13. After the three hostile challenges of Mark 11:27–12:27, the reader might expect the next question to Jesus to be hostile, but this was not a hostile encounter. Earlier references in the gospel to the teachers of religious law have portrayed them as antagonistic (Mark 2:6–7, 16; 3:22; 7:1, 5; 8:31; 9:14; 10:33; 11:18, 27), and Jesus will warn the crowds against their hypocrisy (12:38–40), but this teacher seems positively inclined toward Jesus and even praised him.

14. The frequent repetition of the command to love others emphasizes its importance to the early church (Matt. 5:43–44; 19:19; 25:31–46; Rom. 13:8–10; Gal. 5:14; James 2:8).

15. When the Davidic dynasty ceased to rule, toward the end of the divided monarchy (after the nation divided), the covenant promise centered on a coming one, labeling that person the righteous branch of David. See Isaiah 11:1 and Jeremiah 23:5–6.

16. See Acts 4:1–22; 23:24; 24:10–27; 25:1–26:32 and 2 Corinthians 11:24–25.

17. For further study, see Romans 1:5, 8; 10:18; 15:19, 23.

18. See Exodus 24:8; Zechariah 9:11; and Hebrews 9:18–20; 10:26–29.

19. See John 1:29; Acts 8:32; 1 Corinthians 5:7; 1 Peter 1:19; and Revelation 5:6, 9, 12; 7:14; 12:11; 13:8.

20. Written by Robert Lowry.

21. See Luke 22:39 and John 18:2.

22. See Isaiah 51:17, 22 and Jeremiah 25:15, 17.

23. Isaac Watts, "At the Cross."

24. All modern translations of Mark's Gospel indicate that Mark 16:9–20 is not likely original. For a simple and concise discussion of the reasons, see the *Holman Christian Standard Study Bible.*

Discover
the whole
40 Days
series

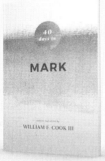

MARK

WILLIAM F. COOK III

1 SAMUEL

DUANE GARRETT

WILLIAM F. COOK III

1 CORINTHIANS

HERSHAEL YORK

WILLIAM F. COOK III

THE
PSALMS

T. J. BETTS

WILLIAM F. COOK III

available
now

available
now

available
spring 2021

available
spring 2021

40daysseries.net